From
Survival
To
Significance

*The How-Tos of Youth Ministry
For the Twenty-first Century*

Troy Jones

WINEPRESS WP PUBLISHING

ISBN 1-57921-130-5
Library of Congress Catalog Card Number: 98-60859

To my wife and partner in ministry,
Jana.
You capture the essence of this phrase,
"Behind every good man is a better woman."

Acknowledgments

- Warren Hassel, my dad, for coming into my life at the age of twenty-two and adopting me. Dad, I am proud to be your only son.
- Dr. Rick Ross, my mentor and senior pastor at Renton Assembly, for investing and speaking into my life in areas where no one else was willing. Words could not begin to express my appreciation and respect for this man.
- Karen Snowden-Jones, my secretary at Renton Assembly for nine years, for being the backbone of every significant ministry at Renton Assembly and being the silent hero when no one was looking.
- Mark Newell, my assistant youth pastor and friend, for being my partner in developing a youth ministry that shook a city for God.
- Diana Kruger, my editor and friend, for spending hours of reading and evaluating the first edition of this book.
- Spring 1998 Northwest College youth ministry class, for spending one semester with me as I wrote this book. Your input, enthusiasm, and ideas have been instrumental in the making of this book.

- Jeffery Portmann, my successor and dear friend, for taking the students at Renton Assembly to a new level. Your attitude and leadership during the transition at Renton Assembly will be a model for the country. Few leaders have the integrity to conduct themselves the way you and Joanne have.

FOREWORD

After being in full-time youth ministry for nearly three decades, I must admit that I have read countless how-to books on youth ministry. But when *From Survival to Significance* entered my hands, the first chapter let me know that it was far from normal.

I recommend it highly.

Troy Jones has captured the magical combination of pragmatic insight and spiritual motivation. He outlines a clear strategy and deals with the real issues people in youth ministry face on a daily basis. Even more crucial, Troy's life, ministry, and integrity gives weight to every sentence he writes. He is one of those rare people in youth ministry who has chosen to have more than a *name*, but to have a *voice*. Consider yourself fortunate if a copy of *From Survival to Significance* has crossed your path. It is a gold mine of inspiration and how-tos for youth ministry in the twenty-first century.

JEANNE MAYO
Cross Current
Youth & Young Adult Ministries
Rockford, Illinois

ENDORSEMENTS

"For eight-and-a-half years I have watched Troy and Jana learn and live out these principles. Part of the success of Renton Assembly is due to not only its youth ministry, but also Troy's tremendous leadership. Every senior pastor should buy this book, read it, and then give it to his or her youth pastor."

—*Dr. Rick Ross, Senior Pastor*
Renton Assembly

"*From Survival to Significance* provides a wonderful tool for anyone working with today's young people. It is biblically based and philosophically sound. It provides fundamental principles and practical steps to implement them. The youth pastor/leader will be challenged, encouraged, and inspired as he reads this book. Author Troy Jones has translated his own broad experience working with students into a how-to manual that will have application well into the twenty-first century."

—*Dr. Warren Bullock, Superintendent*
Northwest District, Assemblies of God

"We live in an age where people know more and more about less and less, striving for information while abandoning revelation. I am embarrassed by this new generation of communicators, who trust in technology and not theology. With all of our ingenious, creative ways of reaching and teaching people, God still sides with the foolishness of preaching to save the lost. May we forever understand that God does not anoint machines, He anoints men and women who are dedicated and devoted to His superior project: mankind.

"Troy Jones is one of those people. He has shifted into a gear that transcends the way we've always done things in the past. His words force us to change the way we will do things in the future.

"As the district youth director, he currently trains countless youth pastors and leaders and provides leadership for thousand's of students in Washington and Northern Idaho. He speaks to us at a time when many have decided to take shortcuts to the road of success. Nothing counterfeit can last forever.

"Allow the reality of these pages the opportunity to take you to the next level. I am eternally blessed to have this man of God as my colleague and confidant. May this book serve as a gift to people and a gratuity to God for the lessons He has taught Troy Jones."

—*Roosevelt H. Hunter*

"Troy Jones has written a book that is a must read for every youth pastor, youth leader, and worker in America. His wisdom and practical insights will help everyone involved with reaching young people to go to the next level of effective ministry."

—*Benny Perez*
Youth Pastor and Evangelist

CONTENTS

Contents

SECTION 2: WIN

SECTION 3: BUILD

SECTION 4: SEND

SECTION ONE
LONGEVITY

INTRODUCTION

My prayer is that God would take the principles of this book and encourage the heart of every leader to make a significant difference in this world. The leaders who truly make a difference in youth ministry are willing to have a longterm commitment to one particular church. So many of us leave just when we are about to be effective. This is why section 1 discusses how longevity and significance go hand in hand. This equation lays the ground work for this first section:

LONGEVITY + CREDIBILITY = SIGNIFICANCE

One of the ingredients of effective churches in America is the *longevity* of the senior pastor. This is even more true in youth ministry. Students will not respond to a fly-by-night pastor. Many young people will never give their loyalty to a youth pastor or leader, because they know he or she will be gone when a "better" opportunity arises.

Let me make it very clear: Longevity by itself doesn't guarantee an effective youth ministry. *Credibility* is earned as we are willing to change and keep fresh. I'm convinced that many people keep changing churches because they are not willing to pay the price to keep fresh. It is easier to go somewhere people won't recognize as quickly the stagnation or lack of anointing.

Longevity combined with laziness, stagnation, and the repetition of old ideas will kill a church. My prayer for every youth pastor and leader reading this book is that God would give you a place to invest years of youth ministry, in order to make a significant difference in students.

Chapter One

The Quest for Significance

—••(0)••—

*Most survive, some succeed; however, only
a few have significance.*
—*Troy Jones*

T his book is written because of my personal desire to make a
difference in this world. So many leaders are discouraged and
defeated because they don't have a dream deep inside. I pray the
principles discussed here will motivate every youth pastor and
Christian leader in America to make a difference in their world.
This book is written to give you practical principles to leave a legacy.

There is a big difference between survival, success, and significance: Most survive, some succeed, but only a few have significance. So many youth pastors and leaders are successful in the
eyes of the Christian world, but they are truly not making a difference. We judge our lives in so many shallow ways: How many do
we have in our group? Am I known in my denomination?

There are real questions we need to be asking: Are we making
a difference in someone's life? What student will serve God for the
rest of her life because of my investment?"

I don't want to *just* survive or even be successful. This is why I
believe in longevity. The pursuit of success is at the root of why
many people bounce around from church to church. It is amazing

how many pastors don't leave a position for *less* money or prestige. God seems to only "speak" when more money or a larger situation comes our way.

Someone once said, "You will never work a day in your life if you find your passion." We need to follow our passion, not the paycheck. My passion in life is to make a difference.

The journey or quest for significance came from the fact that I was raised in a broken home. All my life I had people literally speaking death into me. The doctors told my mother to have an abortion because of the chance of my being mentally handicapped. I went to speech class all my elementary years because of my stuttering problems. I grew up with labels like "retarded" and "bastard child."

At the age of thirteen God put a dream into my heart. I was saved at Cedar Springs Bible Camp in August of 1980. This was the beginning of my quest for significance. That day I decided I wanted to make a difference in my world and that the rest of my life would be committed to Jesus Christ. God took a young boy who society said wouldn't make it and gave him a dream to make a difference.

This book is designed to give you practical how-tos for youth ministry. In the midst of the practicality, don't be tempted to miss the principles enumerated throughout the book. If you are reading this book and you are not involved with youth ministry, take the principles and apply them to any ministry in which you are involved.

The following are four principles of significance in youth ministry—the beginning points to be effective. If you don't catch the principles of this chapter, you'll never have true significance in life. Too many people read book after book, attend conference after conference, and never change, because they haven't come to grips with these four principles.

FOUR PRINCIPLES OF SIGNIFICANCE

1. *Know* your purpose
2. *Show* your plan

3. *Grow* your people
4. *Flow* with problems

Principle 1: *Know* Your Purpose

Youth pastors and leaders who are making a difference know why they exist; they understand their gifts and the calling that God has placed on their lives. One of the greatest challenges we will have in youth ministry as we enter the twenty-first century is determining the *why* of our ministries. Only the youth pastors who determine that will be effective.

So many people have a difficult time following us because we have no idea where we are going. Then the moment we declare our purpose, we go to another conference and change it. When that doesn't work, we hear another good idea and go with that. Don't misunderstand me, we need to change with the times, to hear new ideas, but somewhere along the line we need to hear from God and decide why this youth ministry exists. Once the purpose is birthed deep inside of us, then we are ready to begin youth ministry.

I believe we must have a definite purpose in ministry. I have found there are three biblical mandates for youth ministry. You may use different terminology, but if a youth ministry is not effectively accomplishing these three mandates, it will never have true significance in student lives.

THREEFOLD PURPOSE
1. *Win*: We must win this generation—or someone else will. A youth ministry of significance will see students won to Christ weekly.
2. *Build*: We must become expert builders in the lives of students. We are called to make disciples, not Christians. A youth ministry of significance will have a systematic approach to building students.
3. *Send*: We must release students into ministry. The effectiveness of our youth ministry is not our seating capacity

but our *sending* capacity. A youth ministry of significance will release students into ministry.

The following are some questions to help you evaluate if you have a well-thought-out purpose for your youth ministry.

1. *Can you explain your purpose in thirty seconds or less to a child?* If not, it is too complicated. My purpose for youth ministry is simple: to win, build, and send students to fulfill the Great Commission.
2. *Do you have purpose behind every ministry you do?* If not, get rid of that ministry. If you want to have significance in youth ministry you don't have time to do ministries that don't accomplish your purpose.
3. *Are you duplicating ministries that accomplish the same thing?* This is the most common, deadly mistake we make in youth ministry and in the church as a whole. Every ministry you do should have a distinct purpose. For example, our youth service had a totally different purpose than our Sunday school. (I will discuss this in detail later).
4. *If I randomly asked a junior-high student in your ministry why you exist, could they tell me?* The purpose should be so simple and easily remembered that everyone in your ministry can communicate it.

If you don't have a clear purpose in your ministry, all the resources and programs and how-tos in the world will never help you. Sit down right now and begin to let God birth purpose in your life.

Principle 2: *Show* Your Plan

Most youth pastors and leaders don't have a plan to accomplish their purpose; we have good intentions but no plan. The reason why people are always in the survival mode is they don't sit down and come up with a God-given plan to win, build, and send students. It is at this point that we blow it.

THREE RESULTS OF THE NO-PLAN APPROACH

1. *Discouragement of students.* Students are sick and tired of being challenged to reach their friends without a plan. We tell them to read their Bible, but we don't give them a plan of action. We challenge them to get involved but provide only insignificant tasks for them to do.
2. *Duplicate ministry efforts.* We end up doing the same thing over and over again. No wonder students are bored with our approach.
3. *Doing versus being.* We get in this mode of always doing something for God instead of *being* someone for God. The result is that people become tired and frustrated.

We must show students the purpose and plan of action for the youth ministry. The following is a chart that I have found to be very effective.

As you evaluate this chart you must be able to answer three question in thirty seconds or less if you truly want to be effective in youth ministry. These three questions will determine whether or not you have a plan to win, build, and send students to fulfill the Great Commission. All of these points will be discussed in subsequent chapters.

1. *How will your ministry win students?* What is your plan? What ministries are geared just for the lost? The most

effective way we won students for Christ at Renton Assembly was through our Friday Night Hangouts and illustrated messages.

2. *How will your ministry build students?* What is the systematic process? How does a student begin to grow in your ministry? How does a student go from point A to point B? The most effective way we built students at Renton Assembly was through our Tuesday Night Home discipleship.

3. *How will your ministry send students?* What is your process? How do you train students to take their campus for Christ?

Principle 3: *Grow* Your People

A very easy trap to fall into is the notion that effective youth ministry is based on programs. Let me make it very clear: If programs were the answer, every church in America would be effective. *The only way to have true significance is to grow people.* Programs assist us in growing students if our hearts bleed for them first.

Many youth pastors and leaders like crowds but don't like people. Our hearts need to bleed for young people, parents, senior citizens, and the lost of our community. Youth pastor or leader, search deep down and ask, "Why am I in youth ministry?" If you are in ministry for prestige, popularity, power, or any other reason other than for people, repent right now. Burn-out happens if our hearts are not in the right place.

At times we become abrasive simply because we don't like young people. Do you still like students? Do you still believe in students? If not, either change your heart or change your position. I believe a great man or woman will change his or her heart. Even when we change our positions, our hearts need to *always* beat for youth. It is an unfortunate tragedy that we have senior pastors who can't stand students.

Principle 4: *Flow* **with Problems**

The last principle of youth ministry significance is the ability to not let problems distract you from your purpose. This is a big issue. You may have a purpose, a plan, and may even grow people; but if you can't handle problems, you will eventually burn out in ministry. Most leaders don't live a life of significance, because they let problems sidetrack them.

I guarantee you will have problems in ministry. But the fact is, no matter what I did with my life I would have problems. So how do we flow with problems? The following are four insights that will help.

1. *Get back to the big picture.* Problems are a reminder we need to keep the big picture in focus. Youth pastors of significance know how to see the big picture—the purpose of winning, building, and sending students. They know how to stop and reflect on the reason God has called them.

2. *Get back on your knees.* Problems are a reminder we need God. Problems are an opportunity for God to give you a miracle. Every miracle in the Bible started with a problem. That problem may be the very thing you need to see growth in your ministry.

3. *Get back to the basics.* Problems are a reminder to keep things simple. Youth pastors and leaders who make a difference in life have a unique ability to get back to the basics of life.

4. *Get back to work.* Problems are a reminder we have a lot of work to accomplish. Without problems we would have no ministry. Stop whining, and get up and do something about your problem. My definition of a problem is, "Something I can do something about." If I can't do anything about it, it is no longer a problem but a past memory.

I have seen way too many youth pastors leave a church because of a problem. That is a shallow reason to leave. We need to have enough courage to stick it out. We need to learn the art of flowing with problems. In my time at Renton Assembly I had parents upset at me, youth staff stab me in the back, false accusations, struggles with staff, and very dry moments with God; but I did not get sidetracked. This is a lesson every youth pastor and leader must comes to grips with.

Chapter Two

The Power of Compound Influence

———— ◄◉► ————

> Leadership is influence.
>
> —*John Maxwell*

Money put in a reasonable mutual fund will double every seven years. Why? The power of compound interest.

It is the same with ministers: Your influence will double after seven years of ministry at one place. I realize this may be stated in overly simple terms, but the truth is I was able to do more for youth ministry in my final three years than in my first seven years. I released more youth pastors into full-time ministry, gave more to missions, started over twenty Bible clubs on campuses, did illustrated messages that reached thousands of people, and much more. Also, my wife developed an eighty-voice youth choir.

This was not because I'm more gifted than the next guy but because of the power of compound interest—compound *influence*.

Longevity Earns Change in Your Pocket

Again, longevity plus credibility will result in significance in ministry. We earn credibility by personal growth, relationships developed, and the fruit people observe in our ministries over the years. Over a period of time a leader earns incredible "change" in his or her pocket. We lead and grow an effective youth ministry only when we have enough change in our pockets to do so. Change—or respect—is earned or spent depending on the way we conduct ourselves. *When it is all said and done, people will follow you because of respect, not because of position or title.*

At Renton Assembly I had enough change in my pocket to do anything I set my heart on. Please don't misunderstand me! This credibility was earned over eighteen years of faithful attendance and ministry. Why could I do an illustrated message, "The Day After the Rapture," and get over 2,500 people to show up at three different productions? How could I get away with doing a fireworks display in our brand-new auditorium on New Year's Eve? Why could I raise over $16,000 for Speed-the-Light in one evening at Renton Assembly? Very simple: I spent over eighteen years of my life earning credibility.

The Six-Year Youth Ministry Principle

This next thought will change you if you can realize the "destiny" behind it: Every year after being at one church for six years, the students you graduate will be totally influenced by your ministry for their whole teenage lives. In my ministry at Renton Assembly, I influenced the destinies of thousands of students. I was there when they started junior high, learned to drive, fought with their parents, graduated from high school, went to college, and got married.

Longevity Forces True Growth in Your Life

There is a big difference between having ten years of experience or one year of experience repeated ten times. I realize some people stay at a place and just stagnate; they repeat ministry and never grow.

My conviction is that true growth happens with the people who know us the best. John Maxwell says success is ". . . people that know me the best respect me the most." We can fool people with our strengths if we don't allow them to know us. During my more than ten years in leadership at Renton Assembly, I had to grow. I could have left at the age of twenty-five and simply floated through life on my present strengths. Staying at one place forced me, in a healthy way, to grow.

Longevity Develops Strong Relationships

If you spend your whole ministry life going from place to place, you never really get to know people. Ministry flows from relationships; relationships take time. You are never truly ministering unless you are investing time in people.

Longevity Brings Health of Family

No matter how you look, at it change is hard on a family. As I write this book, I am in the process of becoming the Northwest District Youth Director. This will be our first change after eight years of marriage and ministry together. The change is hard on my wife. We have relationships at Renton Assembly that are strong. There are people at our church who are just like relatives to my two little girls. I think of Candace Ferguson, our church secretary. She has taken our girls under her care. She has invested in our girls as if they were her own.

SHALLOW REASONS TO LEAVE DEEP WATERS

So many youth pastors and leaders never have a significant impact in a church, because they leave when the waters get deep. We tend to say, "God is moving us on." Yet, if the truth were known, we are really leaving the deep waters for shallow reasons. The following are five shallow reasons I would never leave a church. These personal convictions of mine are why I have been at Renton Assembly for over eighteen years and am presently faithfully attending.

Not Getting Along with the Senior Pastor

My heart grieves for youth pastors and leaders who leave because of a poor relationship with the senior pastor. Many times, youth pastors and leaders repeat this cycle over and over again. Don't leave a church because you can't get along with the senior pastor. Instead, allow God to build so much character in you that you become a blessing to him.

Not Getting Paid Enough

While money is a very important issue, I think salary is a shallow reason to leave a church. I'm not a hireling; no one can pay me to do tricks. A principle I have lived by is always work harder than you are paid for, and someone will pay you for it. We will never make a significant impact on our world if we live and breathe for money. Don't misunderstand me; we ministers should be well paid. But the ones who are paid the most live for the passion of ministry, not pay. We also need to get control of the way we spend our money. This is so important that I will deal with it at length in chapter 6, "Give Yourself a Pay Raise."

Conflict with Parents/Students

We need to learn to love conflict. To run from it means we run from an opportunity to grow. If we don't learn to become expert problem solvers, our ministries will be limited. Every conflict is an opportunity to compliment your ministry. We need to learn how to go from complaint to compliment.

One day a very upset mother called and wanted to remove her son from our youth ministry. She was not saved and was very concerned with the way one of my youth staff had related to her boy. I dealt with the problem. Later, she wrote me a note thanking me for caring enough to get involved: "Thank you for getting involved in a very difficult situation. I believe in your church. If there is a

God, He definitely lives at Renton Assembly." This lady gave her life to Jesus and is now an active part of the church.

Greener-Grass Mentality

If the grass is not greener where you are, please don't leave and make it brown somewhere else. Many youth pastors and leaders are what I call *honeymoon seekers*. They are always changing because they are seeking the thrill and energy of a new place.

A Church Doesn't Let the Youth Pastor Grow

I realize this may be a reality at times. Ultimately, if you simply can't grow at a church, you may need to leave. However, many times the reason we can't grow has nothing to do with the people in the church; it has to do with our attitude and perception—and it is just easier to blame others. Changing your environment will not make you grow! *Changing you will make you grow!*

Ironically, I have found some churches won't let us grow because of our attitudes toward our role as youth pastor or leader. Youth pastors and leaders tend to be so tunnel-visioned on youth that it actually becomes a hindrance. This view will kill your effectiveness at a church. It is played out in the way youth pastors and leaders act, talk, preach, and think. We need to focus on youth, but remember to keep your mind on the big picture. The way you view yourself is how others will view you.

> It was he who gave some to be apostles, some to be prophets, some to be evangelists, and some to be pastors and teachers. (Eph. 4:11)

I am a pastor with a burden for youth. I don't even like the term *youth pastor*. Ephesians 4:11 doesn't say that God gave some to be youth pastors; it says God gave some to be pastors. This attitude is very significant to the way we do ministry. If you can catch the spirit of this principle, it will open unlimited areas of growth for you. I have heard people say that youth ministry is not a stepping stone to senior pastoring. I agree. *However, it is the best training ground we have in the church world for senior pastoring.*

WHEN IS IT TIME TO LEAVE A CHURCH?

This is a very difficult question with no simple answers. The bottom line is to leave only when God releases you of the burden for your current place of ministry. We must be careful not to release ourselves of the burden because of lack of money, stressful relationships, conflicts, or the greener-grass mentality. It is my personal conviction to only leave a ministry when all *five* of these criteria are totally in place.

When Everything Is at a Peak

My desire is that whenever I leave a place everyone would say, "He is crazy," because everything is going so well. I would leave with no regrets.

When God Releases the Burden

This is a soul-searching question. Do I want to leave for a better opportunity, or is God truly involved in this? Because these five criteria must all be present in order for me to leave a place, if I feel the burden released, yet my wife doesn't feel that this is a God thing, I probably need to keep seeking God.

When There Is No Bitterness in Your Spirit

Never leave a place with a bitter spirit. Live life without any regrets. Forgive anyone who has hurt you. There are far too many bitter pastors and leaders. Bitterness is a choice.

When Your Spouse Feels Good about the Change

We must be in total unity with our spouses. Don't leave a place until your spouse has the green light, too. This doesn't mean that your spouse doesn't have any uncomfortable feelings, it just means that deep inside he or she knows it is from God.

When You Have the Blessing of Your Senior Pastor

I would never leave a place without the blessing of my senior pastor. We must believe that God speaks through leadership and be willing to walk under authority.

CHAPTER THREE

GROW DAILY OR DIE GRADUALLY

―•(◦)•―

Jesus drew a crowd because everyday he withdrew from
the crowd. We fail because we try to draw a crowd without
withdrawing first.

—*Troy Jones*

Many youth pastors and leaders will never enjoy longevity at a
church, because they lack personal growth. We feel as if
people treat us like little kids. The problem is, many of us act like
kids. We like to make excuses. We blame the pastors, the church,
and the students for the problems that face us. Yet deep inside we
know we are not growing.

Youth pastors who blame are absolutely *lame*.

Stop blaming people for your attitude, the lack of growth in
your ministry, and the lack of adult workers. Stop blaming your
senior pastor for not giving you pulpit time. Stop blaming your
students because they don't know how to pray. A healthy youth
pastor or leader must be growing daily. Grow daily or die gradu-
ally. The reason we don't have effective youth ministries is because
we don't have healthy youth pastors and leaders.

Six Principles for Personal Growth

People with weak foundations don't finish strong. When we face the storms of life, the strength of our foundation will be tested. Many people build their lives on emotions, acceptance by people, spiritual pride, and experience. Inside they are dying; they have no character or convictions.

The following are the top six growth principles of my life. These principles will help you develop a foundation that will last. We will use the acronym GROWTH.

Guard Your Quiet Time

"Very early in the morning, while it was still dark, Jesus got up, left the house and went off to a solitary place, where he prayed" (Mark 1:35).

Jesus deliberately found a place to be alone so he could pray. *Many of us love the ministry more than Jesus.* We cannot allow the demands of ministry to keep us away from times of quietness. Our quiet times give us an opportunity to reflect, set new goals, be refreshed, pray, and meditate on the Word.

Public victories are won in private battles. Without time to be refreshed, we will become shallow inside. We must make an appointment with God. When we have an appointment with someone, we know exactly when and where we will meet. In appendix A, I have provided you with a sheet for making appointments with God.

Right Relationships

Do not be misled: "Bad company corrupts good character" (1 Cor. 15:33).

We become like the people we hang around. This is a truth that has made me who I am today. If we hang around small-minded people, we will become small minded. If we hang around burned-out, negative ministers, we will be negative.

The number one significant principle: Hang out with people who are doing youth ministry better than you. Pride stops us from embracing people who have strengths we don't have.

I believe it is our personal responsibility to find three types of relationships:

- *Mentors*: people who speak into our lives
- *Models*: people who show us how to live
- *Motivators*: people who spark us to action

I have never met some of my greatest mentors, but their books and tapes mentor me. Let me offer one very important piece of advice for developing positive relationships with authority figures that you desire to emulate: *Never make them guess your name.* Always offer your name to them, even if you think they know it.

Obedience to God's Word

"Do not merely listen to the word, and so deceive yourselves. Do what it says" (James 1:22).

The key to personal growth is to obey the Word. I have met people who know how to pray, but they can't control their mouths. You may be able to speak in tongues, but if you don't love your spouse, your spiritual life is meaningless (see 1 Cor. 13). *Growth happens not when you read the Word, but when you do the Word.*

Winning Attitude

God can't help you if you have a negative, pessimistic attitude toward life. I agree with Mark Twain, "There is no sadder sight than a young pessimist."

Because of their attitude, many youth pastors and leaders will never have the joy of longevity. I have met youth pastors and leaders who won't wear a tie in the office, even though they know that would be the desire of their senior pastor. You need to get rid of that poor attitude. You deserve to be fired.

If the truth were known, people leave church or are asked to leave way too early because of their attitude. *Your attitude will determine your altitude.* People can criticize and belittle me, but they can't take away my attitude. My attitude is a choice!

I believe that most of us are one attitude away from accomplishing great things for God. Don't let an attitude keep you small. Don't let an attitude keep bitterness in your heart. Don't let an attitude keep you stagnant. Don't let an attitude force you to leave a church.

Teachable Spirit

Whoever loves discipline loves knowledge, but he who hates correction is stupid (Prov. 12:1).

I want to challenge you with one of the most honest questions you will ever ask yourself, *"Am I a teachable person?"* We need to be like a sponge and soak things in. The fact that you are reading this book demonstrates that you are teachable.

Teachable youth pastors and leaders are always:

- Reading books
- Asking questions
- Taking notes
- Listening to tapes
- Exhibiting an eager attitude to learn
- Embracing people who are doing it better than they are
- Learning from their senior pastor
- Listening to their spouse
- Consistently changing in their personal lives

Perhaps the most important principle in this book is: We must be teachable. If Moses hadn't accepted teaching from his father-in-law, Jethro, what would have happened to his ministry? (Exod. 18). Many youth pastors and leaders are like concrete: They are all mixed up and permanently set. They allow spiritual pride to "set" in.

Heart for Purity

God has called us to purity in every area of our lives. Many of us stop growing because of a lack of purity. We need to have a commitment to purity in five significant areas of our life:

- Mind
- Ministry
- Marriage
- Money
- Motives

It is a mistake to think purity is something we must only preach to our students. Somehow, when we become adults nobody challenges us to purity. Abstinence is a short-time commitment; purity is a lifetime commitment. Abstinence includes only one part of your body; purity includes every part of your body. The Scripture never calls us to sexual *abstinence*, but to sexual *purity*.

Many ministers have stopped growing and have fallen because of this area. If you are struggling in any way, you need to find a Christian friend to help you get back on your feet.

Chapter Four

Insights on Integrity

———⊷•((◉))•⊶———

> Integrity is the glue that holds our way of life together.
> We must consistently strive to keep our integrity intact.
> —*Billy Graham*

Without integrity, personal growth will be stifled. Many youth pastors and leaders move from church to church because of a lack of moral strength.

Let's reflect again on the equation that we discussed earlier:

LONGEVITY + CREDIBILITY = SIGNIFICANCE

Credibility is earned through a life of character. We will never develop the influence to lead unless we live a life above reproach. Paul told Timothy that one of the qualities of a church leader is to live above reproach (1 Tim. 3:2). Nothing will substitute for character. Some hide behind their authority, their gifts, or their success stories. Without personal integrity, your ministry will *never* be effective.

The Word of God makes it very clear that leaders will be held to a higher standard (James 3:1). As a minister you must have credibility in three areas of your life:

- Ministry
- Marriage
- Money

The next two chapters will deal with credibility in our marriage and money. Let's look at some very specific integrity issues that will impact your whole ministry life.

Northwest District Superintendent Warren Bullock and I have composed a list of integrity issues every leader must avoid at all cost:

- *Riding alone with someone of the opposite sex.* Don't do it, even if it is convenient. Even being alone with someone of the opposite sex is asking for problems.
- *"Borrowing" church money.* Don't ever borrow a dime. I know you plan to pay it back, but it's wrong!
- *Not tithing.* We must pay our tithe not because it is a bylaw, but because it's a Bible law.
- *Entertaining gossip against any leadership.* This includes all staff, denominational leaders, and even political leaders. The test of this is when you don't agree with the leadership. Anyone can be loyal when they agree.
- *Not working a forty-hour week.* On top of that, you should donate the same amount of time that you expect every Christian to donate.
- *Watching questionable tv, r-rated movies, or worse.* When nobody is watching, what are you watching?
- *Not giving an honorarium to a speaker.* If you told someone the entire offering would go to him or her, it better happen.
- *Communicating false numbers.* That leads people to believe you're running what you're not. It's a big issue. We must represent the brutal truth when it comes to numbers.

- *Skipping sessions of a conference your church is paying you to attend.*
- *Using an illustration that is not true, but presenting it as if it was. We should never stretch the truth, even for effect.*
- *Not praying for someone you promised to pray for.*
- *Not returning a promised phone call.*
- *Not paying your bills on time.*
- *Making long-distance personal calls on the church calling card or church phone.*
- *Buying lottery tickets.*
- *Viewing ungodly web pages.*

CHAPTER FIVE

SKIN AGAINST SKIN, AND IT AIN'T NO SIN

———◆———

If you can't take care of your bride,
God will not let you take care of His.
—*Author unknown*

The following is written for couples in ministry. If you are single, please read with caution. I will discuss principles that will be very helpful to you one day if marriage is in God's plan for your life. To have significance you must have credibility in these three areas:

- Ministry
- Marriage
- Money

We cannot allow the pressures of ministry to negatively impact our marriage. I have found that many ministers don't have an active and healthy sex life. God has called us to purity. While an active and healthy sex life can't make you pure; the Word of God makes it very clear it is a part of protecting our purity (see 1 Cor. 7).

How does this fit under the topic of longevity at a church? Ministry, marriage, and sex have everything to do with each other.

- Without good sex, we don't have a good marriage
- Without a good marriage, we don't have a good ministry
- Without a good ministry, we don't have longevity

As leaders and pastors, our ministries are based upon us having credibility in our marriages. *If you can't take care of your bride, God will not let you take care of His.*

There is no young person, service, or church that is more important than my wife and two daughters. I realize that some have used their family as an excuse for not working hard or for being irresponsible. Such a leader has an integrity problem as well as a family problem.

It's a challenge to realize that God created men and women totally different from each other. We must honor and respect the way God created each gender. Let's take communication for an example:

- Women communicate with men heart to heart
- Men communicate with women skin against skin

This is not intended to be a complete handbook on marriage. However, from my perspective, we can't truly talk about effective ministry without spending a few moments discussing what we all deal with all the time: mariage and sex. The following is a list of needs that women and men have. Frustration in marriage and sex is often caused from a lack of understanding these needs.

LADIES NEED	MEN NEED
• Love	• Appreciation
• Listening ears	• Active sex life
• Leadership	• Alone time

For Ladies
(written by my wife, Jana.)

Ladies, God created men to communicate through sex. Men are not out of control. It is very healthy for them to communicate through sex. We need to understand that their hearts and spirits are the most open during that time. A wise wife will honor and never belittle a man during sex. Here are the main three things your husband needs from you.

Number One: Your Husband Needs *Appreciation*

Men need to be appreciated. Men will only return to successful situations. If all you do is nag on him, it will become a negative thing in your relationship. Nagging will never motivate a man. Get rid of the "honey do" list. Begin to appreciate your man when he does little things for you. Brag on him behind his back. Stop complaining and downgrading the man God put in your life.

Number Two: Your Husbands Needs an *Active* Sex Life

We need to learn to enjoy sex. It is amazing what will happen to a lady's mindset if she will take some initiative in this area. Attack your man when he is not expecting it. The Scripture makes it very clear that we should do everything we can to be totally available to our mates (see 1 Cor. 7).

Ladies, don't think for a moment that sex is only for men. If you are struggling in this area, I would encourage you to seek out help from a godly woman who is willing to invest in your life.

Number Three: Your Husband Needs Times to be *Alone*

Every man has a cave where he needs time to be alone. We ladies must be careful not to take it personally and think something is wrong when our respective husbands want time to be alone.

He will come out of his cave if you simply put "honey" outside of the cave—a positive home environment, appreciation, and total availability for sex.

For Men

Men, we need a fresh commitment to focus on our families. We need to totally understand that ladies communicate with their hearts. Sex for them begins with a phone call from the office. If your wife is not enjoying sex, don't force her, but be very sensitive to her emotional needs.

The following are the three basic needs of every woman. We must be totally committed to doing everything we can to meet the needs of our spouse.

Number One: Your Wife Needs *Love*

Ladies need us to communicate our love to them. Even though we communicate with our skin, we must learn that sexual fulfillment is done in the context of two people sharing their love for each other. Men, if your wife has lost her sexual drive, it is because she doesn't feel loved.

The way we speak and treat our wives outside of the bedroom is when we communicate love. *Don't ever belittle your spouse.* Never use hurtful words, such as *shut up* or *stupid.* Always speak life into your spouse. Some men have said so many hurtful things to their wives that they can't enjoy sex with them. What goes under your skin goes straight to your wife's heart. This is why I am so careful to protect my wife (and kids) from unnecessary gossip and garbage.

The bottom line to showing a lady love is *giving* her time. On your calendar you should have days off, vacation time, and dates with your wife. When you take your days off don't sleep in. Give your family your best. Why is it that we spend hours planning the next youth activity, but no time planning the next family activity? Ladies need our undivided attention. Jana and I will often get away for the weekend just to be together. It is amazing how our communication improves when we schedule time together.

Number Two: Your Wife Needs You to *Listen*

The greatest thing that a wife needs is for her husband to listen. Don't try to solve their problems. When she is upset, simply let her talk. A man must learn to keep his mouth closed and sincerely listen to his wife.

The best thing we can do is turn the TV off. I recommend that you don't have a TV the first year of your marriage. This was probably one of the greatest decisions Jana and I made. Now, we have only one TV in the house, and we keep it upstairs in an out-of-the-way room.

Number Three: Your Wife Needs You To Provide Spiritual *Leadership*

We have a responsibility to provide spiritual leadership in our homes. To be very honest with you, this has been one of my greatest challenges. Over the years, I have made a choice that I must be the priest of my house. I am convinced that this is a great need in the heart of every woman. Ladies have a deep commitment to holidays, vacations, and family devotions because they want a legacy and memories created in the family.

It is the man's responsibility to lead in family devotions. Every night, we read to our daughters. On Thursday and Saturday evenings before bedtime, we have family devotions. This is probably one of the most difficult things I have to lead in, especially with our girls being so young. In appendix B, I have provided you with a "12-Minute Family Devotional Guide."

Finally have enough confidence to give your wife the freedom to blossom in her ministry. Don't expect your wife to be someone she isn't. When your wife discovers what God has gifted her to do, she will surprise you. Your wife has unbelievable potential. I firmly believe that most men have a gold mine living right in their homes and their ministries would double if they got out of the way of their wives.

CHAPTER SIX

GIVE YOURSELF A PAY RAISE

———⫷●⫸———

Give and it shall be given unto you.
—*Luke 6:38*

If your finances are a mess, I guarantee you will never have significance in life, let alone longevity at a church. We need to get our financial lives in order.

To have significance you must have credibility in your:

- Ministry
- Marriage
- Money

Sadly, many people believe that what they need is a pay raise from their boss to help their financial picture. *However, it's not how much you make, but what you do with what you make that counts.* Every time I make a wise financial choice, I give myself a pay raise. For example, last year, by spending some time evaluating my car insurance, I was able to save $600 a year on insurance. I came home and told my wife I got a $50 monthly pay raise. This is just one example.

This isn't a financial seminar, but if I can get this one principle into your life, the chances of you staying in ministry and at a church for some time will be greatly enhanced.

HOW TO GIVE YOURSELF A PAY RAISE

Be a Giver

I cannot afford not to tithe. Every time I give to God, I give my family a pay raise. You are robbing from God if you're not tithing. The last thing we need are crooks preaching to our youth. Then, above your tithe, give to missions. God's blessing will be yours only if you're a giver.

Avoid Deadly Debt

Make it your passion to have no debt. Before you ever think about buying a house, take care of *all* debt. The very fact that I pay *no* interest on credit cards, college, or car loans means that I make more money than the guy who gets paid exactly what I do but struggles with debt. Also, my house is on a fifteen-year payment plan in order to save interest. Don't even consider buying a house until you have no other loans and you can afford the payments on a fifteen-year mortgage.

Cut Up Your Credit Cards if You Pay One Penny of Interest

Nobody should have more than one credit card. The rule of my house is we allow ourselves one credit card as long as we pay *no* interest—ever!

Invest into an IRA

If you begin as a young adult to simply invest $2,000 a year in an IRA, you will be a millionaire before age sixty-five. Invest 10 percent of everything you make, and you can retire early. Every time I invest my money, I give myself a pay raise.

Spend One Minute of Financial Planning for Every Hour of Work

Every week, spend time with your family budgeting, setting goals, paying bills, and investing money. If I work forty to fifty-five hours a week, I should at least spend forty to fifty-five minutes planning how I will spend my salary. This one minute of planning is the greatest contribution toward a pay raise I have ever made.

Read Financial Books

The few minutes you spend reading can save you an unlimited amount of money. Learning even one principle that saves you money is a great way to give yourself a pay raise.

Don't Buy a Brand New Car

When you buy a car brand new, you are throwing away thousands of dollars. We bought our 1993 Grand Prix for $9,000 less than its original price. It only had 20,000 miles on it. To me, that was a $9,000 pay raise I gave myself.

Don't Buy Big-ticket Items without Thinking about It for Twenty-Four Hours

This rule alone has given me literally hundreds of pay raises.

CHAPTER SEVEN

BEING A KEY PLAYER WITHOUT HAVING THE KEY ROLE

The most important single ingredient in the formula of
success is knowing how to get along with people.
—*Theodore Roosevelt*

P erhaps the single greatest reason youth pastors and leaders don't
enjoy longevity at a local church is they don't get along with
their senior pastor. Frankly, with the right attitude, youth pastors
and leaders can get along with any senior pastor. David got along
with Saul because he made a *choice* to respect God's leadership.
Leaving a church simply because of a major conflict with the senior pastor is a shallow way to hear God speak.

This book will speak to the youth pastors' and leaders' responsibility in this relationship. This in no way suggests that the senior
pastor doesn't have a huge role in this relationship. Senior pastors
need to stop being insecure; they need to pay well, communicate,
trust, and invest in the relationship. However, youth pastors and
leaders can be catalysts for creating healthy relationships. *God has
put you there to be a blessing in your senior pastor's life*. Being a key

player without having the key role means we need to support and lift the hands of the person who plays that key role.

Whatever you sow you will reap later. Be the kind of youth pastor or leader you want one day when you are a senior pastor. *Would you want your youth pastor or leader to have your attitude?*

Understand Your Unique Relationship

There is no other relationship just like the one you have with your senior pastor. It is unique! It doesn't exist in any other field of work. Conflict is natural because your senior pastor wears all types of hats.

HE IS YOUR BOSS

I use the term *boss* very deliberately. I am trying to emphasize that even if you don't agree with him, you must respect him as your boss. As such, he is responsible for work schedules, budgets, office hours, salaries, etc.

HE IS YOUR PASTOR

Your senior pastor needs the respect and honor due your pastor. You can see how conflict sets in so easily: On Friday he is telling you to be on time to the office; then on Sunday he is teaching you to love Jesus with all your heart.

HE IS YOUR FRIEND

I enjoy a friendship with my senior pastor. However, it is very important to understand he is my boss first; second, my pastor; and third, my friend. A healthy friendship cannot be developed without understanding this uniqueness. I frequently hear, "My senior pastor never plays golf with me." Why do I seldom hear, "My senior pastor never asks about my office hours"? We like the friendship part, but not the boss part.

HE CAN EVEN WEAR MORE HATS

If he has teenagers, he becomes a parent. If he is a district official with your denomination, he wears that hat.

SOLVING THE CHALLENGES OF THIS UNIQUE RELATIONSHIP

1. *Understand that your senior pastor is also a human being.* He may be a great pastor but a weak boss or friend. Be OK with that. He may even struggle as a spiritual person but be a great boss. You are there to bless him.
2. *Understand that in one ten-minute conversation he may put on all types of hats.* If in doubt, treat him as your boss!
3. *Call him "pastor" at all times.*
4. *Build healthy relationships with his wife and children.* Derrick and Karissa Ross were an active part of our youth ministry. I made it my business to involve them, love them, and build a great relationship with them. They are both great spiritual leaders in our youth ministry. Every kid needs special ministry. Our pastor's kids don't deserve any less. Also, if you don't get along with his wife, you can eventually kiss your job goodbye—like it or not, that is reality.

Be Loyal at All Times

To me, disloyalty is grounds for dismissal at a church. Proverbs 22:1 says, "A good name is more desirable than great riches." If we destroy the good name of our senior pastor, God will hold us accountable. We need to be loyal, both privately and publicly. If we have a problem, we need to follow the Bible and have enough guts to talk to our senior pastor one on one.

SUBTLE WAYS OF DISLOYALTY

1. *Listening to someone say you preach better than your senior pastor.* When you preach only a couple times a year, of course they will say that. If this goes to your head or if you enjoy listening to this, you have a shallow life and deserve to be fired.

2. *Entertaining prayer requests for your senior pastor's spiritual life.* Enough said. Don't listen! This only breeds pride in your own life.
3. *Keeping your resignation in your back pocket.*
4. *Not being trustworthy.* You need to be a trustworthy youth pastor or leader. Always be totally honest with your senior pastor. Be ethical in every decision you make.
5. *Preaching something you know goes against his biblical understanding.*

Be a Pastor

Look at yourself as a pastor specializing in youth ministry. Don't act like a kid without any concern for the life of the church. Why should a senior pastor let you preach on Sunday night when he knows you will make a fool of yourself?

BEING A PASTOR MEANS . . .

- *Earning respect from adults.* Learn and enjoy preaching to adults.
- *Dressing appropriately.* A good rule of thumb: Follow your senior pastor's lead. He may not have enough courage to tell you how to dress, so simply follow his example. Many youth pastors think they need to look like their students to be effective. I am not against looking sharp. But students respond best to adults who love them and are willing to be *themselves.*
- *Caring about the life of the church.* Care about the children's ministry, Music Department, senior citizens, etc. At our last Family Fall Fest, I personally showed up one hour early to help set up.
- *Showing up early on Sunday morning.* With our first service beginning at 9:00 A.M., my whole family was at the church by 7:35 on Sunday mornings. As a pastor, I care about Sunday morning, and I need to be there to make a difference.

- *Encouraging youth to be at church on Sunday morning.* Your students need to hear your senior pastor preach. They need to see you taking notes, saying "Amen," and enjoying the service.
- *Being a problem solver.* Learn how to identify a problem and solve it. The most valuable person in any organization is a person who learns how to identify and solve a problem.
- *Working fifty-five to sixty hours a week.* While we must be careful not to overwork nor underwork, I believe we have a responsibility to put in fifty-five to sixty hours a week. I get paid for the first forty hours and the rest I donate to the church as I expect any Christian to do.

Learn to Take Monkeys Off His Back

A "monkey" is any responsibility that jumps on the back of your senior pastor. Find those monkeys your senior pastor doesn't enjoy—and *kill* them. Develop a sincere servant attitude toward your senior pastor. Don't kiss up, but do serve! Over the years of working with Pastor Rick Ross, I took care of his kids, housesat, drove him to the airport, watered his yard, ran errands, and made it my business to kill any and all monkeys I could find at the church. I took the initiative to find out what bothered him and dealt with it.

HOW TO MEET MONKEYS

1. *Ask him.* Let him know you are there to do anything for him. Be sincere. He will be able to see the difference between a servant and a sucker.
2. *Listen at staff meetings.* At our staff meetings on Tuesdays, I would listen to what might be frustrating him. Learn to listen and read between the lines.
3. *Use common sense.* If your pastor is vacuuming in the foyer, grab the vacuum. If he is setting up chairs, grab a couple of students to help.

Refuse to Entertain Any Negative Comments

Your mission is to make your senior pastor look good. No matter how great your senior pastor may be, there will always be someone ready to make a negative comment. You must watch the back of your senior pastor.

HOW TO WATCH THE BACK OF YOUR PASTOR
- Refuse to let people *compare* your ministries
- Refuse to let people *critize* your pastor
- Refuse to let people *complain* to you

Publicly express support for the senior pastor. Regularly, I would make sincere statements about Pastor Rick and Susan from the pulpit. People knew I was the last person to complain to; I simply wouldn't listen.

Overcommunicate with Him

Most conflict between groups of people is not a generation gap, but a communication gap. We all struggle with communication. As youth pastors and leaders, you must become experts in the area of communicating with your senior pastor. Many of our senior pastors are weak in this area themselves. There are creative ways to communicate even to the most difficult person.

CREATIVE WAYS TO COMMUNICATE
- *Go places with him on his agenda.* Go with your senior pastor when he runs an errand, visits the hospital, attends a district event, etc. The best talks Pastor Rick Ross and I had together were in the car. Life is so busy. Quit whining that your senior pastor doesn't have you and your wife over for dinner. Hang out with him on his agenda, not *yours.*
- *Write FYI (for your information) notes to him.* When you do a flier, put it in his box with a short FYI note. Even though he knows you will be on vacation, leave him a reminder

note a couple of days before you leave. Little notes will make a big difference

- *Set up appointments.* If you can set up a weekly or biweekly time with your pastor, that would be great. Pastor Rick and I never had an official time, but we did have healthy communication (most of the time).

- *Utilize the hit-and-run method.* Most youth pastors and leaders use the head-on-collision approach with the senior pastor. They back their senior pastor in a corner when he is not ready for it, and say, "God told me to turn our sanctuary into an activity center. Can I do it?" The head-on-collision approach will only leave scars on your body—people have died because of it.

  Instead, use the hit-and-run approach. Walking down the hallway, I would say, "Pastor Rick, I have an idea I would like your thoughts on." Then I kept walking. Then one day as he was leaving the office I said, "There are churches that are doing great outreaches on Friday nights. Talk to you soon." You are doing this not to manipulate, but to prepare him to respond to your new idea. The goal of the hit and run is to get a healthy discussion going, not to get your way.

- *Keep a list of things to talk to him about.* Many youth pastors and leaders, once they get the attention of their senior pastor, mumble and waste time. We forget what we wanted to communicate because it was two weeks ago. Keep a list! Believe me, your senior pastor will appreciate this discipline.

- *Right timing.* Right timing is everything. There were days I definitely knew it wasn't the right time to present Pastor Rick with my new idea of how to reach the world. Sunday morning before he preaches is a bad time to tell him that the parents in the youth ministry are ticked off. If you present a great idea at the wrong time, you may close the door on that idea forever.

Be Financially Responsible

One major reason senior pastors are frustrated with their youth pastors and leaders is they feel as if they don't care about money. Youth pastors and leaders need to be experts in the area of financial management. Youth pastor and leader, listen: You will kill yourself, you will kill your relationship with your senior pastor, and you will kill any hope of longevity at a church if you don't learn how to make and keep a budget. Again, to have *significance* we must earn credibility in the way we deal with money.

The best financial advice I can give you is: Overbudget your expenses and underbudget your income. Most youth pastors and leaders work opposite of this principle, and they get into trouble.

Catch His Vision and Complement It

Your ministry needs to complement the ministry of your local church, not compete with it.

In no way am I suggesting that the youth ministry has to be an exact duplication of the church. Nobody wants that. Reaching students has unique challenges and opportunities. We need to fight for unity in vision even though we have variety in approaches.

The reality is that many feel their pastor has no vision. He may have no vision in writing or he may be very discouraged, but something brought that man of God to the ministry—and it is your responsibility to fan that into flame.

CHAPTER EIGHT

DO MORE BY DOING LESS

I don't know the key to success, but the key to failure is
trying to please everybody.

—*Bill Cosby*

We must think how we can organize our lives and ministries so that we don't burnout after the first three years at a church. God has called us to be marathon runners, not ten-yard dashers! As youth pastors and leaders, if we are just going from event to event, running around with no direction, we will never stay at one local church. We must deliberately make some healthy decisions so we can make a significant impact on people.

There are three types of youth pastors or leaders:

1. The *survivalist*: He or she hopes to get by.
2. The *successor*: He or she desires to get ahead.
3. The *significanct*: He or she is purpose driven and wants to make a difference. He or she organizes for longevity.

The following are eight ways to organize your life and youth ministry to make a significant impact on this generation. You are the only one who can organize your life.

Determine What Only You Can Do

We must determine what only we can do and develop leaders to do the rest. Bill Gates believes he really has only two jobs. Number one is to cast a vision. Number two is to motivate people to fulfill it. As a youth pastor, I realized the three things I had to do, and I attempted to give them my full energy. Depending on the size of your church and the giftings God has given you, those things will differ. The three things I put my energy on are as follows:

1. *Casting vision.* Once a year in February, I would cast before the church the vision for the youth ministry. And at least every thirty days I would cast the vision before the youth staff or while I was preaching.
2. *Developing leadership.* This was also my responsibility. We will give more thought to this in the "Send" section of this book.
3. *Preaching the Word.* So often we get so busy we forget that one of our main responsibilities is to preach the Word.

Determine What Evenings You Will Not Do Church Ministry

I just talked with a youth pastor who was busy five to six nights a week. The only way to have longevity at the church is to do ministry no more than four evenings per week. As a youth pastor, I rarely scheduled ministry on Monday, Thursday, or Saturday nights. These were my nights with my family. Rick Warren suggests doing ministry only three nights a week. I realize that when doing camps and missions trips, this is difficult. But fight for it as much as possible.

Determine to Take Time Off

I am very dogmatic about taking my day off. Longevity means we must pace ourselves. My philosophy is: Work hard, relax hard.

Rick Warren does three things to refuel himself. He has a lot to teach us about longevity.

1. *Divert daily.* Do something that's fun.
2. *Withdraw weekly.* Don't compromise your day off. This is your Sabbath; you need it! Many youth pastors and leaders try to take Fridays off. I don't recommend this in youth ministry. There are way too many interruptions. Friday is a key day for students.
3. *Abandon annually.* Take your vacation, and don't call in. I suggest you don't take a vacation during July or August. Your summer is busy enough. To help during the summertime, I take my vacation at the end of May. Even if you have to take your kids out of school for a couple of days, avoid taking your vacation during July and August. We always found May and December to be good months.

Determine Boundaries around Your Life

There is no way for me to overemphasize this point. We must establish healthy boundaries in our lives. The following is a list of questions to help you think of some boundaries in your personal life.

- *How often will you preach outside of your church?*
- *How many weeks will you be gone during the summer?* I'm a firm believer in Bible camps, missions trips, and choir tours. During the summer, we are gone more than any other time of the year. That is fine, but it can be easily abused. Limit your summer absences to no more than four or five weeks. With a little creativity this doesn't have to mean ever missing four or five Sundays and Wednesdays. We are in this ministry for the long haul; don't kill yourself and your youth ministry during the summer.

- *What evenings will be my family nights?*
- *What is my day off?*

Determine to Simplify Fundraisers

Youth pastors and leaders kill their effectiveness and longevity at a church because they don't have a grip on their fundraisers. For example, I would never sell Christmas trees again. We made decent money, but the pain and turmoil weren't worth the income.

FIVE GUIDELINES FOR FUNDRAISERS
1. *The fewer, the better*. I suggest no more than three a year. My last year of youth ministry, we did one fundraiser for youth ministry expenses and two for missions/Speed-the-Light.
2. *Make significant money*. Avoid fundraisers that make only a few hundred dollars (i.e., car washes)—you could save that time by writing a check yourself. Find fundraisers that make significant money.
3. *Definite beginning and ending*. Find fundraisers that can be done between one day to one week. Don't let them drag out. Some of you are still collecting money from that crazy candy-bar sale a year ago.
4. *Raise money from the community*. Fundraisers that bring money from the community are ideal and are better than those in which your church people have to participate. However, missions fundraisers work best with the church body.
5. *Develop annual fundraisers*. Find two or three good fundraisers and build on them from year to year. The best ones we ever did were fireworks stands. It met all the criteria of a good fundraiser.

Determine to Tweak Your Week

The vast majority of our ministry times were done on Sundays or Wednesday nights (midweek service). We need to realize that we will burn the students out if we try to provide something for them every night of the week.

SCHEDULING TIPS

1. *Move the youth choir to Sunday morning during Sunday school.* Our youth choir grew to over eighty students, and it freed up our Sunday afternoons to do our youth staff and student leadership meetings at 4:00 P.M.

2. *Schedule ministry times before the midweek service.* We did drama, worship practice, prayer meetings, Bible quizzes, and phone calls all on Wednesday nights from 5:30–6:30. At 6:30, everyone joined the prayer meeting for a final prayer time together. Then at 6:40 we all greeted new people.

3. *Combine junior and senior high during midweek.* I realize this is not possible, or even advisable, for some situations; but there is no doubt in my mind that the strengths outweigh the weaknesses. We addressed those weaknesses by simply creating the best of both worlds. At times we ministered to the whole youth ministry, and at times we did specialized ministry to meet the needs of junior high and senior high students. Here are the strengths:

   A. Students enjoy crowds.
   B. Only one worship team has to be developed.
   C. Students don't have to change pastors at ninth grade.
   D. It gives the senior high a chance to minister to the younger generations.
   E. It simplifies the youth ministry schedule. I planned a healthy, weekly youth ministry schedule—one that has at least three nights free and one that effectively wins, builds, and sends students. In appendix C, I have provided a sample of our youth ministry schedule.

4. *If possible, preach only once a week.* The youth pastor or leader should do the vast majority of the preaching at the

midweek service. He should also spend his time training people to teach and lead on Sunday mornings. I realize this is not always possible, but your aim should be to pastor by walking around on Sunday mornings. You will stay fresh if you only preach the midweek youth service. Your students will appreciate hearing a different voice.

Determine to Organize Your Personal Life

Many youth pastors and leaders actually have a weird pride about being disorganized. This is an attitude of failure. We must do everything we can to organize ourselves. There are many books on this subject. I will present just a few thoughts on organization. Your chaotic life is your responsibility. Do something about it today.

HOW TO ORGANIZE YOURSELF
1. *Deliberately say yes and no.* Every time I say yes to any commitment, I am saying no to something else; when I say no to a commitment, I am saying yes to something else. I am not overly into time management. I believe strongly in event management. I save myself countless hours simply by saying no to what God hasn't called me to do.
2. *Return phone calls/e-mails.* One of the simplest pieces of advice I can give you is to return your phone calls immediately. The following is a scale I use to determine how sharp my organization skills are:

Calls returned that day:	SUPERIOR
Calls returned within one day:	EXCELLENT
Calls returned within two days:	GOOD
Calls returned within three days:	OK
Calls returned after three days:	UNACCEPTABLE

3. *Keep your desk clean.* Work on one thing at a time.

4. *Make a daily to-do list.* Every day make a to-do list. Follow that list, and get things done step by step.
5. *Begin filing today.* Begin filing sermon notes, research for future messages, and ministry items. Every time I read a book, I list on the back of the book what I want to file. When I am done I make a copy and file it.
6. *Pick a time and place to have daily devotions.* In appendix A I have provided a sheet to help you make appointments with God. If you don't organize your devotional life, you will have no life.

SECTION TWO
WIN

INTRODUCTION

If we are not seeing students won to Christ each week, we are simply a scouting club. Now is the time to get rid of a club or group mentality and develop a thriving ministry. We are not called to be people pleasers; we are called to be soul winners.

There is a big difference between a youth group and a youth ministry. A youth ministry reaches students; a youth group entertains students. A youth ministry gives; a youth group spends. A youth ministry worships; a youth group sings. A youth ministry impacts a world; a youth group pampers a student. A youth ministry releases students; a youth group counts students. A youth ministry has a full church focus; a youth group has a "youth group" focus. A youth ministry dreams the impossible; a youth group settles for the possible.

We all need to ask ourselves an honest question: Am I leading a youth ministry or a youth group? My personal passion is to bury every youth group in America and resurrect youth ministries that will reach a generation.

If we are not winning students to Christ, we are simply a group with an ineffective us-four-and-no-more attitude. We must have a definite strategy to reach the lost. Our youth ministries must be built around this passion.

Each section of this book will build on this diagram.

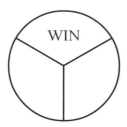

"Jesus said, 'It is not the healthy who need a doctor, but the sick'" (Matt. 9:12–13). Jesus makes it very clear that His sole purpose in coming to the earth was to call sinners to repentance. Many churches have a self-righteous attitude toward the lost; they would be shocked if a real sinner walked through the doors. I believe that an effective church will see cigarette butts in the parking lot and occasionally hear swearing in the lobby. When we lose our passion for the lost, we lose everything. If people are not getting saved, we might as well close our doors.

In Acts 2:47 the Bible says that the Lord added to the church daily and that the early church was praising God. They were not being *seeker sensitive*. I strongly believe that people will get saved when the Word is preached with conviction and the presence of God is evident. Yes, we need to be sensitive to sinners. However, this does not mean we need to hinder our worship and the message of the Word.

CHAPTER NINE

QUIT ASKING THE WRONG QUESTIONS

---=)((O))(=---

*If you ask the wrong questions, you will get
the wrong answers.*

—*Anonymous*

Many of our youth ministries are dry and mundane because we haven't seen a soul won to Christ for years. New life creates excitement and energy. The greatest antidote for burnout is seeing a real, live sinner changed by the power of God.

In some ways the church-growth movement has hurt our youth ministries and churches as a whole. We have people telling us how to grow a church who have never done it themselves. The emphasis is on numbers; so many of our youth ministries are big but not effective. Rick Warren says, "Size is not the issue. You can be big and healthy or big and flabby. You can be small and healthy or small and wimpy. Big isn't better; small isn't better. Healthy is better."

I am not against counting. But I am convinced that most of us are guilty of counting the wrong numbers. All we seem to care about is how many we have in our midweek service. This number has value; however, let's be honest: Our pride causes us to count the wrong number and compete with each other. The number God cares about is not how many come to the midweek service, but how many are not coming from the community. We need to begin to count the right numbers and not get lost in the world of church growth.

It is shallow and egotistical to determine the health of our ministry by merely counting how many people show up on Wednesday night. This would be like getting on a scale every week to determine if we are healthy. A scale gives *limited* knowledge. More important questions would be, What is my blood pressure? How many times a week am I exercising? What is my heart rate? Do I have cancer?

The scale makes many of our youth ministries report a good number; but in many cases, we are dying of cancer and don't realize it. If we ask the wrong question, we will get the wrong answer. The following are twelve questions that I believe will help any youth pastor and leader acheive an honest evaluation of their ministry's health.

QUESTIONS TO DETERMINE SIGNIFICANCE

How Many Students Are Truly Being Saved Each Week?

If students are not getting saved, then no matter how many people attend, you have cancer in your ministry.

How Many Campus Missionaries Are Active on the Local Campus?

The greatest mission field on the face of the earth is the local school campus. If you are not effectively releasing your students to impact their campuses, you are not being effective.

How Much Money Are You Giving to Reach Your Community for Christ?

You spend your money on what is important to you. How much money do you spend advertising to your community? How much money do you spend on specific outreaches in your church?

How Many New People Have Become an Active Part of Your Youth Ministry in the Last Six Months?

New life creates energy. If you are not effectively winning new people, then there is a disease.

How Many Students Attend Prayer Meetings?

To me this was a very important question. If all I was doing was drawing a crowd that did not know how to pray, then I knew my ministry needed CPR (Christ, prayer, and repentance).

How Many Students Attend Your Midweek Service?

If this is the only question you ask, then you don't understand the true meaning of youth ministry. However, if this number is not growing, it does indicate a health problem. If my two little girls did not grow, I wouldn't demand that they grow. I would take them to the doctor and find out what was wrong with them.

How Many Students Are Involved in an Effective Small Group?

Sometimes you can't grow because you don't have an effective way to keep the harvest that God is giving you.

How Many Students Are Involved with Discipleship?

We are called to make disciples. It concerns me that at a youth pastors' conference some get impressed with those who have large numbers and never even ask about who is involved with discipleship.

How Many Adults Are Actively Involved with Your Ministry?

This question reveals why many youth ministries are not growing. A ministry will never grow beyond the leader's ability to motivate a team around him/her.

How Many Students Are Involved with Ministry?

The health of your youth ministry is determined by how many students you have in the game, not by how many are watching from the bleachers.

How Many Full-time Ministers Are You Training?

I believe that every minister should be training and motivating others to be involved in ministry. This is one of the greatest signs of health.

How Much Money Is Your Church Giving to Missions?

If your youth ministry is not giving to missions, then you are not a youth ministry. It is a shame that many of us spend more money on fuel for our vehicles than we give to missions. This is a definite sign of disease.

The remainder of this book will give practical thoughts on how to effectively deal with these questions. I pray that God would stir our hearts and we would begin to ask the right questions about our youth ministries.

CHAPTER TEN

THE MOST IMPORTANT
NIGHT OF THE WEEK

Don't use your people to build a great work; use your
work to build a great people.

—*Jack Hyles*

The most important night of your week is your youth service. If
you have a poorly planned youth service, don't even think about
starting a new ministry. It is amazing to me how we always want to
start something new when what we're presently doing is ineffective.
I need to become an expert builder in my youth service. The students who faithfully attend my youth service deserve a service of
quality and excellence. They deserve a service that will build them.

I can tell a lot about a person's ministry by the way they conduct themselves in their service. I have been to many youth services where I would be embarrassed to bring an unsaved person.
The energy is low; the environment is just weird. We need to do
whatever it takes to have a service of excellence. Students want
excellence and a place of celebration.

The following are ten principles on how to build effective youth
services.

Principle 1: Determine Philosophy

We must determine the reason why we have our youth services. If we don't know the purpose of our times together, we will be tossed by every latest fad. We need to be purpose driven in everything we do.

The purpose of an effective youth service is found in Acts 2:47: ". . . praising God and enjoying the favor of all the people. And the Lord added to their number daily those who were being saved." I recommend that your youth service be designed in such a way as to *build* students. The two environments most effective for building students on Wednesday nights are:

1. *Environment of celebration.* In Acts 2:47 the Bible says they praised God and they enjoyed being together. Earlier in Acts the Bible says they devoted themselves to the apostles' teaching (see 2:42). An environment of celebration must be cultivated in (*a*) anointed and contemporary worship and (*b*) biblical and contemporary preaching.
2. *Environment of evangelism.* Notice the Bible says that as they praised God the Lord added to their church. It doesn't say they watered down the gospel so nobody would be offended. When there is a definite celebration in your service based on contemporary worship and preaching, students will get saved weekly.

I realize this is a philosophy question and many arguments and debates have taken place over this issue. My conviction is that students who need Jesus will get saved in our services if the power of God is present. *We must be careful not to be so sensitive to the lost that we become worthless to everyone.* I am totally convinced that the unchurched will line up to get saved if our students are fired up for God and if they love Jesus passionately. Many have become so wishy-washy or super-sensitive that neither the believer is changed nor is the unbeliever attracted.

If our students don't know how to worship and if they are not in love with the Word, we don't have anything to offer the unchurched student. As I have studied youth services across this country that are seeing students saved regularly, I have observed the following characteristics:

- Students are early for prayer
- Students bring their Bibles
- Students bring their friends
- Students love to worship
- Students are taking notes on messages

Youth pastors or leaders who have an entertainment mentality may draw in crowds, but they have no church. These characteristics don't happen just by accident. They happen because youth pastors and leaders have determined *why* they are having services. They have determined to build their youth services on something that will last.

Beware of the temptation to entertain students. Beware of becoming so sensitive to some people that you are ineffective with everybody.

Principle 2: Preach the Word

Paul told young Timothy to preach the Word. Don't preach your thoughts, don't preach on the latest fad, and don't preach topic after topic. Preach the *Word*. You may preach in an expository manner or topically, but you must teach students the Word—the only foundation that will last.

At the end of every message give a chance for students to give their life to Jesus Christ. Excitement will come to your youth ministry when the students see their friends get saved.

So you say, "If I preach the Word to Christians, how will the unchurched get saved?" The whole New Testament was written to believers, but people get saved daily by reading it. The Word of God has power to draw people to their knees.

Principle 3: Worship with Excellence

You must teach and provide your students with an environment of celebration. If you want to develop an effective youth ministry, you must worship with excellence. Worship will unite students and give them a sense of purpose.

Music is very important in the life of a teenager. So we must master the art of training our students to love praising God and worshiping Him. Now, to be honest with you, I have very little music ability. My wife, Jana, is a gift from God, and she provides the leadership in this area. No matter what the size of your ministry, the resource you may have, or the talent in your group, worship can become a vital part of your services.

Jana and I have put together this list of practical insights to help in the area of worship.

INSIGHTS ON WORSHIP
- *Keep it simple.* Allow God to use your gifts, don't try to imitate anybody, and begin with whatever resource you may have. I would encourage any youth pastor who has a small desire to learn the guitar to do it. With this simple skill you can lead in worship at any time.
- *Involve students.* Students love to see other students leading them in worship, and it's a great opportunity to release students into ministry.
- *Be organized.* There is no excuse for lack of organization. No matter what resources you may have, be organized with them. At 6:59 is no time to be looking for that overhead.
- *Develop a practice time for worship.* We did our practice on Wednesdays at 5:30 P.M. I recommend doing the practice one hour and thirty minutes before service begins. This gives one hour for practice, some time for prayer, and time to greet new people before the service.
- *Speak life into the students.* One of the most common mistakes I see is youth pastors or leaders standing in front and

implying nobody in the room loves worship. When we see one student worship God, we need to celebrate. See, speak, and treat your students like you want them to be, not like they might be.

- *Teach new songs.* Be careful not to overdo this, but your students need new and updated worship songs.

Principle 4: Provide Ministry Time before the Service

The more people who arrive early for church and are involved with hands-on ministry, the more effective your youth service will be. See appendix C for my full youth ministry schedule. Before our Wednesday night services, we offered a number of ministries.

- Ministers in training (MIT)
- Worship practice
- Phone calls
- Warfare prayer
- Setup
- Church Express (bus ministry to pick up students)
- Drama practice
- Bible quiz practice

All of these ministries concluded by 6:30 P.M., and everyone would join the prayer meeting. This was a time to unite right before the service. At 6:40, everyone involved with these ministries would go out and greet our new people. Once we started at 7:00, our students were ready to begin.

Principle 5: Develop Big Days

Big days are key dates during the year when you reach out to your city for God. They can be anything from illustrated messages to special theme evenings. There are some definite advantages to having big days:

- *They give students something to rally around.* It's an easy way to bring friends to church.
- *They break growth barriers.* When you have a big day, it is your opportunity to show your students how many you can effectively run. It shows them the potential for growth.
- *They are soul-winning tools.* An effective youth ministry will see students get saved weekly. The strength of big days is to see a significant number get saved at one time and stir up the vision to see the same thing happen every week.
- *They are advertising tools.* Big days make it very easy to advertise your youth ministry.

One idea is to try to have back-to-back big days. Every fall, around Halloween time, we held an illustrated message called "To Hell and Back." Then we would bring in a speaker, such as Roosevelt Hunter, for our following service. This gave our young people two healthy opportunities to invite their friends to hear about Christ.

Principle 6: Demand Excellence in the Service

Don't be sloppy. Avoid being a perfectionist, but develop a spirit of excellence. Students will appreciate excellence. Some may think that just because this is a youth service they can relax in this area. That attitude may be exactly why the service is not growing.

COMMON AREAS YOUTH MINISTRIES BECOME SLACK IN
- Starting the service on time
- Chewing gum publicly
- Trash and garbage not picked up
- Having no one at the entrance to greet students before and during the service
- Sound system/overhead projector not working properly
- A service schedule that is not thought through

- Shutting the entrance so new people or those who walk in late feel uncomfortable
- Allowing students to sit while everyone else is standing
- No directional signs to communicate where the service is being held
- Allowing distractions in the service
- Involving people in the service who don't have a clue
- Everyone not knowing the service order. It is very sloppy to have someone yell, "Pastor Troy, who is next?"

Principle 7: Deal with Distractions

We must have enough courage to deal with any and all distractions. Youth pastors and leaders complain all the time about young people who are not listening and those who write notes. If you don't deal with those distractions, you deserve to have those problems.

FOUR STEPS TO DEALING WITH DISTRACTIONS

1. *Warn them*. That's first. Be very specific, smile, and be simple in your instruction. When you warn them, look at them straight in the eyes and let them know you will not tolerate the particular behavior. Communicate clearly that this is God's house and if they continue to distract, you will not hesitate to move them. I may talk to a student once before I begin this process in my mind. (Most of the time, when this is done correctly, it will handle the problem. In all my years of youth ministry, I rarely had to go to step two. But believe me, there were times . . .)
2. *Move them*. After you have given them a simple and specific warning with a smile and they don't change the behavior, then you need to move them. Typically, I would just move them to the back of the room. The goal is to do this without any distraction to the service. Move only one person at a time, and sit them by a leader. Move the influencer who is causing the problem. At this point, make it very clear that if they distract the service again, they will have to leave the room.

3. *Remove them.* After you have moved them and you continue to have problems, you need to remove them from that specific youth service. This rarely happens if you follow this three-step process. However, when it does, you need to have the courage to follow through.

4. *Restore them.* I have found that the greatest way to restore students who have caused problems is to build a relationship with those young people throughout the week. Take that young person out for a hamburger and tell them they are valuable to you. In my ten years at Renton Assembly there were only a few times I had to permanently remove anyone from the youth ministry.

Principle 8: Win Your New People

If we are not effectively reaching the new people God is giving us, why should God give us others who we won't reach? This question needs to wake us up. Most churches are not even reaching the fish that are jumping into the boat, let alone the ones outside the boat.

I am convinced that every youth ministry has more new people walking into their church than they think. Stop for a moment and do a quick calculation of how many new students walk into your church per year. The following chart will help you do this. Calculate how many new people come approximately every week to the following events. Be conservative. I think you will be amazed at the results. I have allowed for down days; that is why I only put forty weeks.

Midweek service	_____ x 40 weeks	=	_____
Sunday morning church	_____ x 40 weeks	=	_____
Sunday school	_____ x 40 weeks	=	_____
Sunday evening church	_____ x 25 weeks	=	_____
Activities	_____ x 8 events	=	_____
Outreaches	_____ x 4 events	=	_____

I hope this exercise helps you see that we have a ton of new people walking through our front doors. I realize they are not all lost, but I guarantee a bunch of them need Jesus Christ. Quit talking about winning the world if you can't begin to impact the ones God is already giving you.

HOW TO WIN NEW PEOPLE

1. *Lay out the red carpet.* Have students at the front doors greeting new people and offering to sit by them. All your youth staff should be at church twenty minutes early just to watch for new people. We ended our prayer meeting twenty minutes before the service and had a VIP (Very Important People) time. Every week, I encouraged the prayer warriors to greet and love new people.

2. *Establish a three-minute rule.* Let your students know that three minutes after the service they are allowed only to search out new people. They won't all do it, but it keeps the vision before them.

3. *Giving honor during the service.* We publicly recognized the new people, and the students would go nuts. Then we gave all the new people and the friend they came with free pizza and soda pop during the middle of the service. This allowed all of them to fill out a new-person card and a chance to meet some friendly and enthusiastic leaders.

4. *Develop a week-long strategy.* If you don't effectively follow up on new people within one week, you have lost them. Here is the plan we used after someone visited on a Wednesday night:

THURSDAY:	Letter from the youth pastor (see appendix D)
WEEKEND:	Phone call from youth staff
TUESDAY:	A home visit, if located within target range
WEDNESDAY:	Phone call from student leader

5. *Call the student who invited the friend.* On Tuesday, call the young person in your ministry who invited the friend, and let them know you are proud of them for inviting their friend last week. This speaks life into them and encourages them to bring that friend back.

Principle 9: Strive for Continuous Improvement

This principle was the number one reason we had an effective youth service. Continuous improvement simply means that every week I would improve in one little area. I would carry a pad of paper with me, and I would write down a continuous-improvement list. Every week, one little thing would be better. No one else may have noticed it, but I would.

I have led in over five hundred youth services at Renton Assembly. One improvement every time helped each service become more effective. The improvement may have been in my preaching, in the way we greeted new people, maybe in the way announcements were given, how my messages were prepared, or how much I prayed for my messages; but one little improvement must be made.

Principle 10: Creatively Bring Unity to Your Ministry

Group dynamics are so important to a youth ministry. Young people want to feel like they belong. They want to feel that there is a sense of family and excitement in the group. Let me give you a number of ideas for bringing a healthy group dynamic to your youth services.

- *Play music before and after the service.*
- *Be available before and after the service.* The most important time of your week is fifteen minutes before and fifteen minutes after your youth service. Youth pastors and leaders must be available to students to love on them, talk with them, and let them know that you will be there for them.

- *Speak life into your students.* Don't get up there and begin to tell people to shut up. Don't ask where everybody is and draw attention to the fact that you may be low in attendance. Speak into the students what you want them to become.
- *Think about your chair setup.* If you expect fifty students to attend, set up only forty-five chairs. People love to see chairs being set up.
- *Be faithful.* Many youth pastors and leaders tend to miss their youth services in the summer. This will kill your group dynamics.
- *Walk slowly through the crowds.* The worst thing we can do during our midweek service is to be in a hurry. Learn to walk slowly and look students in the eyes as you talk to them.

CHAPTER ELEVEN

GETTING *US* BACK ON THE CAMPUS

———◦《◉》◦———

Attempt something so impossible that unless God is
in it, it is doomed to failure.

—Author unknown

The greatest missionary field in the world is the local school campus. If a youth ministry is not involved with reaching the campus, it's not really a ministry. The campus provides us with a platform to reach students. I'm excited about this section because I'm going to share with you simple insights that I wish someone would have shared with me early in my ministry.

It is amazing to see how the doors have opened on campuses throughout America. In my early days of ministry, campus ministry was difficult and hostile. One of the most important cases concerning campus Bible clubs that was argued before the Supreme Court originated in Renton during my time as youth pastor at Renton Assembly.

Even in the midst of this hostile environment, God opened up the doors. More than ten years after I began youth ministry, the schools are now calling us to speak in the classrooms, provide lunch monitors, and do seminars. Our campus missionaries have established twenty Bible clubs, which have impacted our community for Christ. Through campus ministry we are reaching more students for Christ than we could ever fit through the doors of our local church.

The following are eight simple and practical ways to make a campus ministry an overall missions strategy of your local church. These are lessons I learned by making many mistakes.

Do Not Demand Your Rights

If someone had taught me this early on, it would have saved me years of struggle. I entered youth ministry with the attitude that the local school had to let me on its campus. This attitude hindered my effectiveness; but over the years, God dealt with my attitude. No matter what the law says or what Christian rights we may or may not have, we must *earn* the right to be on the campus. We earn that right simply by being servants.

Just as a youth staff member has to earn the right to lead in your youth ministry, so it is on campus. The schools need responsible adults who can relate to youth. I don't care what rights you may have when you walk on my turf Wednesday night. If I don't trust you, I will deal with the problem. When they find out who we really are, they will call us.

Here are some ways to earn the right to be on campus:

- *Be a servant at all times.*
- *Check in with the administration every time you walk onto the campus.*
- *Have a definite reason to be on the campus.* For example, you may be on campus to advertise with the school newspaper. Take your time as you walk around the campus. If someone begins to look at you strangely and question you, the worst thing in the world is to be unprepared with an answer as to why you are there. Simply introduce yourself and explain that you are looking for the ASB office that handles the newspaper.
- *Build relationships with the administration.* Administrators are the key to being on that campus. In some ways, we are

in the same business: helping students. The administration needs to become your partner, not your enemy.

- *Don't talk about God on the campus.* This is a time to build relationships with the students, not talk about God. After trust was built, I was able to periodically mention I was a pastor. If in doubt, don't say anything that may put undue stress on your relationship with the administration.

Establish Student Campus Missionaries

The greatest opportunity a student has in his or her life is to be a campus missionary. We must do everything possible to equip and release our students on the campus. The Assemblies of God and other organizations have published all types of excellent tools to help with establishing students as campus missionaries. See appendix E for names and more information.

ESTABLISHING CAMPUS MISSIONARIES

- *Have students fill out an application.* When students fill out an application, it builds credibility and a sense of ownership for the program.
- *Send a letter of acceptance to the campus missionary.* Once you have received an application, put together an acceptance letter for the student. Again, this gives the student a sense of ownership. It would be helpful to even have the senior pastor sign the letter.
- *Honor and pray for the student.* Sometime in the month of September, have a commissioning service in which you pray for and anoint the student with oil.
- *Establish a Bible club on campus.* Do everything you can to assist the student in beginning a Bible club on his or her campus.
- *Develop monthly meetings.* Once a month meet with your campus missionaries for a time of encouragement and training. We did this the first Sunday of the month during our student leadership meeting.

Focus on One Campus at a Time

Focusing on an individual campus is very important, especially if you represent a variety of campuses in your youth ministry. We had over fifty campuses in our youth ministry. Having so many tended to paralyze our efforts. However, I remember the day that I personally decided to go after only *one* school—Renton High School. This was the beginning of our effectiveness.

To determine which school to begin with, choose:

- *The school where you have students who want to make a difference.* If you don't have students on that campus who are ready to reach that school for Christ, your efforts will be limited.
- *The school closest to the church.* It is an ineffective church that can send money for foreign missions but never set foot on the campus across the street.
- *The school where you have relationships.* If you have any connections at all with this campus, this is the place to begin.
- *The school that is ripe.* A few schools fought us. I believe we need to find the places where God has already opened the doors. There are definite times when the field needs first to be tilled. We need wisdom from God to recognize which schools have open doors.

Determine a Day for Campus Ministry

If you don't plan for campus ministry, it will never happen. Every youth pastor and leader should have a scheduled time each week to commit to campus ministry. My assistant, Pastor Mark Newell, would go on the campuses every Tuesday and Wednesday afternoon. Our youth staff accompanied him on one of these days. I scheduled Mondays as a day I would speak in classrooms. Earlier in our ministry I would give Friday afternoons to campus ministry.

There are so many creative approaches. Once you begin this process, you will find the doors will fly open. Here are a few:

- *Speak in classrooms.* Have your students refer you to their teachers. I loved speaking on campus. I would speak on financial management, goal setting, and ethics in the business world. Even though you can't make direct references to the Bible, the impact you have on the students and your Christian youth is very effective.
- *Lunchroom monitors.* Every week, we sent up to twenty adults from our church to help at lunchtime. The principal appreciated the fact that young adults took time out of their day just to hang out with students—and do it for free.
- *Sporting events.* We would often show up at students' games just to encourage them. At the time, they may not say how much it means to them, but later on they will come back and tell you what an impact it made on their life.
- *Advertise in the school newspaper and yearbook.* I used this tool every year. First of all, it gave me a great reason to be on campus. But it also provided the students a platform for inviting their friends to church. This will cost some money; but if we're saying we believe in evangelism, we should put our money where our mouth is.
- *Tutoring and/or teaching.* Again, this is a great way to get on campus and reach the students on their turf.
- *Volunteer to chaperone.* Every school is looking for responsible adults to chaperone at dances or sporting events. As the salt of the world, we need to get out of the shaker and be where the students are.
- *Passing out free soda.* When we first started campus ministry and could not get on campus, I simply passed out free soda pop across the street from Renton High School on Friday afternoons with a flier for our Friday Nite Hangout outreach.

Preach the Heart of Campus Ministry

You get what you preach. We must train and teach our students to win their campuses for Christ. Students must understand that they are either a missionary or a mission field. Romans 10:17 teaches that faith comes through hearing the Word of God. We will build faith in our students through the Word.

HOW TO PREACH THE HEART OF CAMPUS MINISTRY

- *Use summer to train students.* We need to train and prepare our students all summer to go back to their mission field. While at camps, on missions trips, and choir tours, talk about the campus back home as a mission field.
- *Have students share testimonies.* The greatest way to build faith in students is for them to hear a war story from one of their peers.
- *Provide them with practical tools.* Students will come alive if we tell them *how* to reach their campus instead of just telling them to reach it. It is our responsibility as pastors or coaches to provide the necessary tools for our students. Some great campus ministry tools are available today. If we don't make them available to our students, we are failing to effectively do our job.

Unite with Other Churches

This may be difficult at times because of our busy schedules, but the more we unite with other churches, the bigger the impact we will make. The greatest advantage of "See You at the Pole" (SYATP) is the uniting of churches.

Uniting with churches takes on different forms, depending on the situation. However, if there was ever a reason for churches to unite, it is campus ministry.

- *Be involved with "See You at the Pole."*
- *Meet with other youth pastors and leaders in the area.* I know life is busy and we have many meetings on our calendars. However, if you can meet together even a couple of times a year, this would greatly enhance your effectiveness.
- *Don't worry about doctrinal issues.* The only issue should be salvation through Jesus Christ. It is very advisable not to even discuss issues that have divided us over the years.
- *Teach your students to unite with other Christians.* Let them know that they need to work and pray together with other believers. Actually, our students will have no problem with this if we model the right attitude.

Use "See You at the Pole" as a Catalyst for Campus Ministry

I believe one reason that campus ministry has exploded in recent years is because of SYATP. This event alone has changed the face of campus ministry. Use this as a catalyst for your campus ministry. Here are some insights I have learned in using this event:

- *Train your students for this outreach.* The greatest mistake we make is to assume that the students will know what to do when they get to the pole. It is our responsibility to train them before the actual day. SYATP has some training material that can assist you in this.
- *Provide resources and advertisements for the students.* SYATP provides T-shirts, buttons, and all types of literature to advertise this event. Use the resources in your services to build momentum. If the students make some of their own signs and banners, it can add a great flavor to the day.
- *Involve the whole church.* This event gives you a perfect opportunity to involve the whole church. Cast the vision in your church bulletin and newsletter. Encourage the church to pray and show up at a pole.

- *Help the students organize their Bible clubs before the outreach.* Club members should have a good idea of when and where they will meet. Assist them in having fliers available that advertise the Bible club at the beginning of a week. The students should also have information cards available, to help get the names and addresses of everyone who attends.
- *Do an all-city rally before SYATP.* This is great way to unite with all the other churches. If there is no rally going in your area, take the initiative to organize one.

Provide Outreaches on a Local Church Level

It is a mistake to do your campus ministry without actively tying it into a local church. Any organization that doesn't unite with the local church is only spinning its wheels. We must provide outreaches that make it easy and natural for the campus missionaries to invite their friends to church. We must actively think of ways to pull the fish into the boat. This is why I believe youth pastors and leaders need to step up to the plate and give leadership on the local school campuses.

OUTREACHES THAT HELPED OUR CAMPUS MISSIONARIES
- *Friday Nite Hangout (FNH).* The success of this event was due to our campus missionaries.
- *Wednesday Night Breakthru.* While our services were mainly directed toward Christian students, every week we saw students get saved. Many of the salvations could be traced somehow back to our efforts on the campus.
- *Activities throughout the year.* These gave our students a safe environment in which to invite their friends to our youth ministry.
- *All-church outreaches.* Train your students to take advantage of all-church outreaches. Encourage them to invite the families of the students they are trying to reach.

CHAPTER TWELVE

THE NIGHT I WAS ARRESTED

———◄◉►———

Early to bed,
Early to rise.
Pray against hell,
And advertise.

—Troy Jones

T he greatest outreach we ever did was Friday Nite Hangout.
For almost a decade we invaded our city with the gospel. While
this was one of the most effective outreaches, it did cause our church
some problems. Later, in discussing problems with this event, I
will communicate one of the worst nights of my life: the night I
was arrested.

When I started FNH, I had no idea the impact it would make in
our area and, later, across America. Countless FNH-type ministries
have been started as a result of the unbelievable results we saw.

In the greater Seattle area alone, thousands of teenagers are
being reached on Friday nights through activity centers such as
FNH: Overlake Christian Church in Kirkland, Washington, began
an FNH-type outreach, and they see well over 800 junior highers;
Eastridge Christian Assembly in Issaquah effectively reaches over
300 students through their Friday night outreach.

As you can see, the Friday Nite Hangout concept is very effective. The amazing thing is that the concept is so simple: Any church of any size can begin a Friday night activity center or simply join hands with a church that is already doing one. The concept of FNH is as simple as a church opening its doors on certain Friday nights throughout the year and providing a place for students to hang out. During this time, activities are offered and a brief gospel message is given during halftime.

The following are key insights on issues a church truly come to grips with to have an effective activity center.

How to Cast the Vision

The church as a whole must catch the vision of reaching students on Friday nights. When the adults enter the church on Sunday morning and see the soda-pop stain on the rug, they must understand the vision. It is amazing how much the church will support reaching students if the people understand the vision of reaching the community. Many of them will never show up, but they are willing to give, invite the youth in the neighborhood, pray, and donate items.

CASTING THE VISION
- *Share your vision and heart to the senior pastor first.* This idea may take him some time to adjust to. Don't get discouraged. Allow him time to process the information and ask questions. He may even want to call another senior pastor of a church doing FNH. Be confident; if God truly wants you to have an FNH, He will direct your pastor. If your pastor has a check in his spirit, allow this to be God's leading in your ministry.
- *Share your vision and heart with the board.* Once your pastor agrees, it is time to get excited about the next step. When talking with the board, communicate that it is an evangelistic outreach. Also, let them know that you will

be a problem solver. Discuss finances—as agreed upon by your senior pastor.

- *Do your homework.* Many times we don't get the support of the leadership because of the way we approach them. If a question comes up that you can't answer, simply communicate that you will get back to them with the information.
- *Share testimonies about other FNHs.* Share positive reports with your leadership and church. People love to hear war stories. This allows them to know that others have effectively done this ministry.
- *Have key leaders visit an FNH.* Countless church leaders visited our FNH throughout the years. Some brought video cameras so they could show their boards and churches what the ministry was like.

How to Count the Cost

We must be willing to pay the price to win the lost. One of my ministry slogans is, "Win the lost, whatever the cost." Sadly, most churches are not willing to pay the price.

Two different cost factors you must keep in mind are the *emotional* and the *economical* costs. There is no way a church can totally count the cost, but the following are some thoughts to help you take an honest look at a great beginning.

EMOTIONAL COSTS

- Is the church ready to give up its entire building on ten to twenty Fridays a year?
- How does the church respond to the fact that weddings and other events will be impacted by FNH?
- Is the church ready for the wear and tear on God's house?
- How will the church respond to critics who say that basketball, video games, and loud music are not appropriate for church?

- Is the church ready to commit some of its best leadership?
- Is the church ready to have lost students come Sunday morning as a result of FNH?

ECONOMICAL COSTS

Please keep in mind that there are many variables that will determine the actual costs.

- *Startup costs*: Beginning costs approximately $5,000. This includes advertisement, equipment, food, staff T-shirts, bracelets, signs, etc.
- *Storage container*: A storage unit, if needed, could cost over $2,000.
- *Per event*: Each event costs approximately $1,500. This includes three inflatables, the upgrading equipment, food, rental of games, etc.

The following are some ideas and sources of income:

- *Café*: A café could bring in $200–$500 per event. If managed correctly, this could be a big help in financing the event.
- *Student fee*: Some churches charge for FNH, and others don't. I have done it both ways, and I personally think charging is better because it allows you to let new people in free, gives students more ownership, and helps the financial picture.
- *Church budget*: I would add about $5,000 a year to my budget for FNH.
- *Fundraising*: Be careful to go easy on this one. We did one fundraiser a year, which was our fireworks stands. The community loved to buy fireworks from an organization that was helping students.
- *Financial donations*: People love to give to a dream. Many people have come and just handed me a check for FNH. One day at the grocery store, a complete stranger gave me a check for $500. We were also able to receive donations from

United Way because anyone in our church or community could earmark their United Way money for FNH.

Involve Students

Students will support what they create. Do everything you can to have student involvement. Present this activity center as a campus outreach. Communicate that the only way for this outreach to be successful is to have the total involvement of the Christian students. At one point in the history of FNH, I learned a lesson the hard way: Due to the fact that I was not involving students effectively, the crowd very quickly became composed almost entirely of unchurched youth. Having over 500 students at an outreach without the support of Christian students is a setup for disaster.

INVOLVING STUDENTS IN THE OUTREACH

- *Involve them in advertisement.* Supply lots of posters and fliers for them to give their friends at school.
- *Involve them in setup and tear down.* In order to be student leaders our youth were required to be at set up for FNH by 4:00 P.M. We would make some exceptions but kept them limited.
- *Involve them in brainstorming ideas.* Students have great ideas if you give them a platform to share them. At times they will give an off-the-wall idea, but that idea may spur the best idea ever thought of concerning FNH.
- *Involve them in running the event.* Allow your students to actually help out at the different events.

Prepare for Problems

As leaders, we must learn to love problems. Problems are a sign of growth and effectiveness. Pastors who have no problems are taking no risks. An activity center of that nature is a problem waiting to happen.

We must be committed to taking immediate action to solve every problem this outreach creates. Don't even consider doing an activity center unless the church and staff are willing to deal with the problems that come along with it. In almost nine years of FNH, our problems were limited because we quickly took action when a problem began.

COMMON PROBLEMS
- Broken windows and doors
- Soda pop on carpet
- Smoking and drinking in the parking lot
- Christian criticism for "compromising with the world"; we had video games and laser tag
- Fights and gang activity
- Disrespect by students

With proper leadership, any problem can be effectively dealt with. The leadership must establish some simple yet effective rules. Here are some rules to consider:

- No coming and going from the event
- No gang activity allowed
- No drinking, swearing, or smoking
- No fighting or violence of any kind

Let me share with you a very extreme example of the problems that can come with an event of this nature.

THE NIGHT I WAS ARRESTED
For the first three years of FNH, things went fairly smoothly. However, at the beginning of 1992, we started to experience gang activity and racial tension. The vast majority of our crowd was African-American, at-risk teens. Tension grew between the rockers and the skaters. I knew we were in a situation that only God could help us out of.

One night, I was attempting to remove a student when the chaos started. Before I knew what was happening, a drunken father jumped out of his car and screamed that he wanted to kill me. My leaders jumped in front of me to save my life. Within moments, six police cars arrived and lined up on the street. An officer read me my rights and arrested me on the spot for allegedly assaulting a kid. Students were throwing rocks at police cars and local restaurants. They were cussing and fighting and kicking each other.

The next day, newspaper headlines read: CHURCH HAS HOUR-LONG STREET RIOT. This whole event was the talk of the city. People either hated me or loved me.

My pastor was on a missions trip, so the first time I saw him was on Sunday morning, two days after the event. The newspaper was in his hand, but he didn't say a word to me. He stepped to the pulpit that morning and what he said explains why FNH was successful. He said, "Good morning! How many of you read the newspaper about Friday Nite Hangout? I want you to know we believe in our students. As long as they spell Pastor Troy's name correctly, let them print the news. We can't buy advertisements like this." Our pastor and the church were committed to problem solving.

Over the next six months, I learned more about problem solving than any other time in my life. All charges against me were dropped, we removed the students who were the bad apples, we put stronger leadership into place, and we met with the government and police to talk policy and establish some ground rules. Six months later, that same newspaper ran another front page article titled CHURCH SOLVES PROBLEMS.

I don't believe this story represents what will happen in your situation. However, it underscores the fact that the church must prepare to solve any problem that this outreach may create.

Advertise in Every Way Possible

The Friday Nite Hangout's success is found in the principle of advertising. Prepare to spend. Over the years, Renton Assembly became known as "The Home of Friday Nite Hangout." Every time you advertise this outreach, you are indirectly advertising the whole church. I can't begin to tell you of the countless people who have attended Renton Assembly because of hearing about FNH.

WAYS TO ADVERTISE
- Full-color posters on every campus
- Thousands of fliers available for students
- Bulk mailing to community
- Huge 20' x 6' banner on street
- FNH Web page
- In-house advertisement: Creatively use your church bulletin, newsletter, and announcements
- Skits and drama
- Big advertising balloon on church building
- School newspaper
- Local news story on FNH
- Distributing free soda pop with fliers outside a local campus

SIX-TO-STICK PRINCIPLE
People must hear something six different ways for it to stick with them. Let your imagination flow. There are many ways to advertise with or without a lot of money. Again, if we believe in the lost, we will spend money to reach them.

Determine the Details of the Event

There are many logistical questions you must research. Brainstorm with your church. The more you can think through before you begin to build support, the better.

QUESTIONS TO THINK THROUGH
- *What age level will you let in?* For years we made the event available to seventh through twelfth grade. Just recently we effectively split the age levels. From 6:00 P.M. to 9:00 P.M. is for sixth through ninth grade only, and 9:00 P.M. to midnight is for ninth grade through college age.

- *What time will you be open?*
- *Which Fridays will you be open?* We were open the first and third Fridays all year around. When we moved to our new facility, we changed to the second and fourth Fridays throughout the year, taking December, July, and August off as a break. Some have effectively done this outreach once a month, taking December and the summer months off.
- *What rooms at the church will the outreach use?* Basically, the entire church was available to FNH. This impacted weddings and other church activities.
- *Where will your storage be?* At one point, I even gave up my office for storage. Eventually we had to buy a storage container.
- *Will you charge the students an entrance fee?* We had free admission. But when we moved to the new facility I added a $3 cover charge. The students took more ownership when they had to get in. This also allowed us to let new people in free.
- *What will you call the event?* Many great names are available. Feel free to use "FNH."
- *Who will be the leadership?* Assemble together an adult leadership team for this outreach. Our event required up to sixty adults to effectively run the entire evening.
- *What will your rules be?* The rule of thumb is this: Keep rules simple, but enforce them.
- *What will be your cleanup procedure?*
- *What activities will you provide?* You don't have to come up with all the activities before you open your doors. The following are some of the activities we provided over the years:

  A. Basketball and tournaments
  B. Volleyball and tournaments
  C. Arcade room with Nintendo, pool, foosball, ping-pong, etc.
  D. Laser tag arena
  E. Outdoor skate park
  F. Café and espresso bar

G. Three different inflatables at each event

H. Limbo activity

Develop a Standard of Excellence

Students will appreciate a standard of excellence. They will not come back if they see a hokey church activity, with dated and broken equipment. When they see the foosball table missing a man, that sends a loud message that nobody cares. Don't let things become slipshod.

RULES OF EXCELLENCE

- *Don't accept donations of items unless they are new or almost new.*
- *When things break down, either fix them or throw them away.*
- *Rent as much as possible.* When we were doing an event a limited number of times per year, renting actually saved money. For years, we bought our Nintendo machines and games. I can't tell you how many times I had to give the games away because they became outdated so quickly. I figured out I could rent twenty games and ten machines each FNH—and get totally updated equipment—for less money than always trying to keep up with the latest changes.
- *Make continuous improvements each FNH.* Don't allow one FNH to go by without improving at least one element.
- *Don't allow outdated items to be a part of your event.*

Develop a Halftime

The heart of FNH is to see students get saved. Halftime was the opportunity to present a short gospel message—the most important element of the evening. Without it, FNH would have become just a great event.

IDEAS ON HALFTIME

- *Hold it at the midpoint of the evening.* It breaks up the evening and gives the students a chance to arrive. We did two halftimes when we divided the junior- and senior-high students: one at 7:15 P.M. and the other at 10:15 P.M.
- *Keep it between fifteen and twenty minutes.*
- *Give out door prizes.*
- *Use drama and human video.*
- *Only give announcements that relate to that particular audience.* The only two announcements we gave related to FNH and our Wednesday night services.
- *The youth pastor or leader must be seen.* The students will begin to recognize the youth pastor or leader.
- *Begin a couple of big-ticket items immediately after halftime.* We would do our laser tag arena and basketball tournaments right after halftime.

SECTION THREE
BUILD

INTRODUCTION

So many youth pastors and leaders burn out and have ineffective youth ministries because they have not learned the art of passionately building students for Christ. The temptation is to build large youth groups and not worry about the depth of the students' lives. Three passages of Scripture have greatly influenced my approach to youth ministry.

> Then Jesus came to them and said, "All authority in heaven and on earth has been given to me. Therefore go and make disciples of all nations, baptizing them in the name of the Father and of the Son and of the Holy Spirit, and teaching them to obey everything I have commanded you. And surely I will be with you always, to the very end of the age." (Matt. 28:18–20)

The only way you can have a great youth ministry is by following the Great Commission Jesus gave us, which is to make disciples of all nations. The word *make* implies a systematic process, a conscientious decision to do something. *Christians are born; disciples are made.* If we are not making disciples, we are being ineffective in youth ministry.

> It was he who gave some to be apostles, some to be prophets, some to be evangelists, and some to be pastors and teachers, to prepare God's people for works of service, so that the body of Christ may be built up. (Eph. 4:11–12)

In this passage, Paul said God gave some to be pastors to prepare God's people for works. The word *prepare* implies a systematic process. We don't prepare students overnight. If you don't have a plan to build students, your ministry is unbiblical and shallow.

> By the grace God has given me, I laid a foundation as an expert builder, and someone else is building on it. But each one should be careful how he builds. (1 Cor. 3:10)

In this passage, Paul says he was an expert *builder*. So many of us desire to be expert preachers, but we haven't given any attention to becoming an expert builder. It takes much more than great preaching to build a great church. The analogy of being an expert builder reveals some amazing insights to our ministries. As an expert builder I must:

1. *Develop a good set of blueprints before I build.* Can you imagine trying to build a house without blueprints? Yet that is how many of us run our youth ministries.
2. *Lay a strong foundation before I build the house.* Many of us like to frame the "houses" of young people, but we don't like to build the foundations. The reason for this is that framing is fun and very visible work, while laying a foundation is very difficult and nobody ever sees it. When is the last time someone walked into your house and complimented your foundation?

CHAPTER THIRTEEN

STOP PREACHING LIKE A YOUTH PASTOR

———⸎«(◉)»⸎———

I go out to preach with two propositions in mind. First, every
person ought to give his life to Christ. Second, whether or not
anyone else gives Him his life, I will give Him mine.
—*Jonathan Edwards*

As youth pastors and leaders, we need to learn the art of preaching. The greatest myth that exists in the minds of youth leaders is that students don't want to be challenged. Somehow we believe that we need to give them something to tickle their ears. The strongest and most effective youth ministries in our nation preach the Word and don't get caught up with silly games. Many of us need to stop preaching like youth pastors and begin to preach like pastors who have a burden for students. There is no doubt that at times we need to adjust our terminology and style, but the last thing students want is for you to treat them like kids.

Now don't get me wrong. Some of the greatest preachers alive are youth pastors and leaders. And with a couple of adjustments the effective ones could preach to any adult audience. Paul told young Timothy to preach! (2 Tim. 4:2). It is clear in Scripture that God chose preaching as a means to win the lost. In Romans 10:14 Paul says, "How can they hear without someone preaching to them?"

Big Question 1

How do I preach to Christian students and unchurched students at the same time? Very simple: Preach the Word with passion and conviction. There is not one book in the Bible that strictly addresses the lost. However, thousands of people get saved daily by reading the Word. The Word of God preached with passion and conviction will build Christians and challenge the lost.

Big Question 2

How do I preach to junior-high and senior-high students at the same time? Very simple: Preach the Word with passion and conviction. There is not one book in the Bible that strictly addresses a specific age group. However, thousands of people of every age are challenged every day by reading it. The Word of God preached with passion will build every age group.

Also, I recommend that Sunday mornings be organized, so you can address the needs of specific age groups. Create the best of both worlds by having the junior highers alone on Sunday morning and with everybody else at the midweek youth service.

Some may feel that I have oversimplified preaching to students. The power of our preaching is found in the Word. Yes, we need to speak in terms students can relate to. Yes, we need to give specific stories and illustrations when preaching to students. However, any and all illustrations should complement the Word, not compete with it.

Over the years, I have learned four preaching principles. When I preach, I attempt to meet all of the following criteria. I trust that these principles will help us to stop preaching like a youth pastor.

Preach Out of the *Overflow* of Your Life

Every time you open your mouth, you need to be so full of God that words just flow out. Be committed to preaching out of the overflow of your life. Three guidelines I have established are:

1. *Keep your mind full.* If you are always reading a book, listening to a tape, or attending a seminar, you will find preaching a lot easier. When I speak, I want information to gush out of my brain.
2. *Keep your heart soft.* If you always spend time in prayer and fasting, you will find preaching a lot easier. When I speak, I want principles to flow from my heart.
3. *Keep your Bible open.* If you always spend time reading, memorizing, and studying the Word, you will find preaching a lot easier. When I preach, I want the Word to pour out of my mouth.

Preach with an *Outpouring* of the Holy Spirit

Our students need to see the Spirit of God at work, and we need the anointing of the Spirit when we preach. I don't completely understand the anointing. However, I do know the difference in my life when I preach with an anointing versus when I preach in my own strength. Here are two Scriptures I pray every time I preach:

- 1 Corinthians 2:3–4: "I came to you in weakness and fear, and with much trembling. My message and my preaching were not with wise and persuasive words, *but with a demonstration of the Spirit's power.*"
- 1 Thessalonians 1:5: "Because our gospel came to you not simply with words, but also with *power, with the Holy Spirit and with deep conviction.*"

Preach with *Obedience* to the Word

I hope there remains no doubts about my conviction to preach the Bible to students. I strongly believe that a systematic and expository approach is the way to build a strong youth ministry. So many youth pastors and leaders preach on topics and throw in the Word. I preach the Word and throw in the topics. The following are five steps I used in teaching our students.

FIVE SIMPLE STEPS TO PREACHING THE WORD

1. *Preach out of one book at a time.* My goal was to preach and teach four to five books of the Bible a year. One can imagine the foundation this would build in a student after several years. (In the fall we would always study the same material our Bible quiz team was studying.)
2. *Spend only six to ten weeks on that specific book.* Your goal is not to preach verse by verse, but to give your students a general overview of that book.
3. *Encourage students to read that book throughout the week.* I would start every message by asking if the students were reading the Word that week. Every student in our youth ministry was challenged to read the book we were studying and a Bible-reading plan we provided.
4. *In Sunday school classes, have teachers go deeper into the same book.* This keeps your Sunday mornings and Wednesday nights going the same direction. Sunday mornings must have a time for discussion and not simply another message.
5. *Have discipleship groups memorize scriptures out of the book.*

That is how we will build the students of the twenty-first century. You can see that if these five steps are systematically and consistently followed, students learn the Word of God. Again, this approach covers four to five books of the Bible every year.

Preach with *Outrageous* Illustrations

Students relate to personal stories and illustrations. Jesus spoke in parables all the time to illustrate the Word of God. Use illustrations to help students understand the Word of God more effectively.

One of the greatest preaching techniques we used was illustrated messages. God gave us unbelievable favor with our church and community through them. The first one we ever did was called "The Day after the Rapture." This one was so popular we repeated it three times, and over 2,500 people were in attendance at this message. On Mother's Day, we did an illustrated message during both Sunday morning services, with over 1,850 people in attendance. People of all ages, whether lost or Christian, love illustrated messages.

INSIGHTS ON DEVELOPING ILLUSTRATED MESSAGES

- *Illustrate with creative titles.* The title is very important and will draw people in if you come up with the right one. We used titles such as "The Day after the Rapture," "Back to the Future," "Battle for Seattle," "The Hand That Rocks the Cradle," and "To Hell and Back."
- *Illustrate with drama.* Use your students, bring in teams from the local Bible colleges, and even get the adults involved.
- *Illustrate with music.* Music is an effective way to create a mood. We used cassettes and CDs, our youth choir, our human video team, and even our adult choir to help set a scene.
- *Illustrate with video.* There are all kinds of good videos; use them.
- *Illustrate with special effects.* The list of what one can use to create special effects is unlimited: smoke machines, lighting, pyro, laser beams, etc.
- *Illustrate with true stories.* Bring in a surprise guest. One year I illustrated my testimony through drama. It was very effective.

- *Illustrate with preservice attractions.* It's a great way to set a mood. We once staged an auto accident outside, a "dead" person in a casket in the lobby, an entrance into Hell, etc.
- *Illustrate around special times of the year.* For example, every year around Halloween we would do "To Hell and Back." And on Mother's Day we did "The Hand That Rocks the Cradle."

CHAPTER FOURTEEN

THE BIGGER YOU GROW, THE SMALLER YOU MUST BECOME

> People catch our spirits just like they catch our
> cols: by getting close to us.
> —*Anonymous*

To be honest with you, I hesitated in writing this section of this book. The concept of small groups stirs up all types of weird negative images in the minds of youth pastors and leaders. At times, we think of cliques or we simply think of just plain hard work. Many of us have had negative experiences with the cell-group concept. My desire is to show you, in a very practical way, a whole different approach to effective small groups.

God made us with a need to have relationships. Families are God's way of putting everyone into a small group. With the breakdown of the family, the church must find creative ways to assimilate every student into a small group. One of the reasons gang activity is so popular is because students will do anything to belong to a group.

The problem is we often think in terms of only one type of small group. Everyone doesn't desire or need to be in the same type of small group. We need to find as many ways to break students down into small groups as possible. *If a student doesn't fit into some small group in your youth ministry, that student will eventually fall through the cracks.* It doesn't matter how much you follow up or how spiritual the student is, if that student doesn't click"with some group, he will fall between the cracks. The bigger you grow, the smaller you must become. Actually, I had one really big youth ministry with a bunch of small youth groups. We need to become experts at building small groups within a large ministry.

There are at least three types of small groups we must build in our ministries.

THREE TYPES OF SMALL GROUPS

1. *Relationship groups*: to build strong friendships within your youth ministry
2. *Discipleship groups:* to train the students to grow spiritually
3. *Ministry teams:* to involve students in ministry

Your goal should be to get every student in at least one or more of these groups. Let's take a closer look at three of them.

Relationship Groups

The purpose of these groups is to build friendships. All of us choose the church we attend by whether or not we have friends there. This is not unspiritual; we were not created to be alone. Many youth pastors and leaders with good intentions say that young people shouldn't come to church because of their friends. I absolutely disagree. Young people choose their church by what friends they have. So do adults.

The best relationship groups happen naturally. However, we need to think in terms of how to creatively put every student into a relationship group. There are many relationship groups within your youth ministry. I would like to explain the most effective ones we were able to put together—our fellowship groups. We did our fellowship groups on Sunday morning during Sunday school.

A PURPOSE-DRIVEN SUNDAY SCHOOL

Most youth ministries have a pathetic Sunday school program. Even if their midweek service is strong, many times their Sunday school hour is very weak. Our Sunday school was one of the main strengths at Renton Assembly. The reason it was strong is that it had purpose: to put students into relationship groups. During our Sunday school we strategically divided our whole ministry into four groups:

- Junior high
- Senior high
- Youth choir (perfect for getting students involved)
- Young adults

During their seventy-five minutes together they would accomplish the following:

• Fellowship groups	30 min.
• Announcements	8 min.
• Speed-the-Light offering	7 min.
• Refreshments	10 min.
• Teaching	20 min.

The teaching would focus on the book of the Bible that the whole youth ministry was studying. The youth choir would do fellowship groups for thirty minutes and practice the remaining of the time.

ALL ABOUT FELLOWSHIP GROUPS

Again, our youth ministry was divided on Sunday mornings into junior high, senior high, young adults, and choir. Within each of these ministries, every student was assimilated into a smaller

115

fellowship group of eight to ten students and met twenty to thirty minutes every Sunday morning for the purpose of creating relationships. The youth staff served as their pastor.

Using the acronym FRIENDS, the following are seven principles of how to have effective fellowship groups.

FLEXIBLE SCHEDULE

The twenty to thirty minutes you meet in your fellowship group must be flexible. The leader must be sensitive to the needs of the students and to what God is saying that day. At the same time, it is very important to have a sense of direction. Let me give you four steps that will help the schedule of a fellowship group:

1. *Opening prayer: 3 minutes.* This is a short time to get everybody on the same page. In effect, it says, "We are here, and it is now time to begin." The leader or the student leader should pray that God would make your time together effective.
2. *Heartfelt message: 5 minutes.* This is the time for the leader to share from his/her heart in a creative way.
3. *Lively discussion: 10 minutes.* Here the leader asks questions to help the students think about their lives and how to apply the Word of God. The leader should also ask questions that complement the youth pastor's message from the previous week's service.
4. *"Growing people" ministry: 10 minutes.* This is the time to grow the students. Creativity and sensitivity to the voice of God is critical. Here are some ways to grow people during this time:

   - *Pray for students' needs within the group.* Either the leader can pray or you can ask the students to all pray for each other. Don't force anyone to pray if they are not comfortable.
   - *Ask questions about their spiritual lives.* Find out what God is teaching them. Ask them about their Bible reading.

- *Celebrate with students.* If a student has a testimony, let him/her share it, and rejoice together.
- *Sympathize with the students.* If a student is struggling, stop and spend one-on-one time praying with him/her.

RIGHT ENVIRONMENT

The environment is vital! While a challenge at times, we need to do everything we can to keep the environment positive, exciting, and full of energy. A few things that help are:

- *Have fun outside the group.* The more you have fun outside the regular group time, the better the group will be. I required my leaders to do something fun with the group at least once a month. This was the means by which we did the vast majority of our activities.
- *Involve new people.* New people breed vitality into a fellowship group.
- *Involve the students.* Students will have a lot more energy if they are involved. People support what they create. Allow the students to make up the flavor of the group.

INDIVIDUAL ATTENTION

The leader must give each student individual attention within that fellowship group. If you do a fellowship group correctly, not one student within your youth ministry needs to go without ministry. Here is a list of things the leader should know about each student:

1. The student's birthdate
2. The student's school
3. The student's home situation
4. The student's hobbies
5. The student's likes and dislikes
6. The student's involvement in the church

ENTHUSIASTIC LEADER

There is no group without a leader. The effectiveness of a fellowship group is determined by the leadership. We had over twenty groups at Renton Assembly, and we never got to the place where every one was effective. But the ones that were effective were definitely lead by enthusiastic leaders. Every youth staff member was required to be involved.

Jeanne Mayo, Cross Current Youth Ministries, gives three bottom lines to being a great small group leader. They are:

1. Love their guts out
2. Pray your guts out
3. Work your guts out

As we love, pray, and work for students, we will make a difference in their lives. Fellowship groups are a lot of hard work. However, they are worth the investment.

NEVER GIVE UP

There will be times of discouragement and failure. There will be times when you are so frustrated with your leaders, you will want to quit. At these times remember: We must fight for small groups. Never give up!

DISCUSS THE WORD

Do not allow your fellowship groups to become gossip sessions or discussions of the latest fad. Discuss the Word. This is not a time for theology discussions, but a time for application. Discuss how to put the Word of God into practice in a way that supports the youth pastor's sermon from last week.

STRATEGICALLY PLAN TO BEGIN AND END THE GROUPS

This is very important. You must strategically plan when you will begin and when you will end the groups. You need to find strategic times of the year when it's natural to give the groups a break. For example, the month of December is a very natural time to give the groups a break. Also, July and August provide a break time. Giving the groups breaks will help keep the leaders fresh and provides you with a way to naturally break up any group you don't feel comfortable with.

Discipleship Groups

The purpose of these groups is to help people grow and mature in the Lord. Students need to be taught how to pray, how to read the Bible, and how to grow spiritually. The three most effective discipleship groups I found were:

- *Bible quiz team.* This is where students study, memorize, and compete in their knowledge of the Word of God.
- *Tuesday night discipleship.* During the fall and spring of the year, we would hold Tuesday night discipleship groups in different homes. Up to eighty students were effectively being discipled in those small groups.
- *Warfare prayer meeting.* Every Wednesday at 6:00 P.M., I personally met with the students to pray. This was a time we taught students how to pray by showing them how to pray.

Ministry Teams

The purpose of a ministry team is to help students use their gifts for God. The best way to build students is by involving them in ministry. A student who does not get involved in ministry will become critical, cynical, and will eventually backslide. I will discuss this whole concept in the "Send" section of this book.

Here are the five most effective small groups within our ministry team:

1. Human video team
2. Worship team
3. Drama team

4. Student leadership team
5. Illustrated message team

The students who were involved with these teams were the core of our youth ministry. The key to helping someone become the core is getting them involved in a ministry team.

Chapter Fifteen

Discipleship Makes or Breaks Your Students

Therefore go and make disciples . . .

—*Matt. 28:19*

Many incorrect images come to mind when we think of discipleship. Some look at it as just a program. Many think of it in terms of youth ministry only. Too many of us have made it a bunch of rules. In this section, my desire is to redefine *discipleship*. Discipleship is not a program. Discipleship must become a lifestyle.

Discipleship is simply showing someone else how to follow Jesus. As youth pastors and leaders, we are called to build disciples. The Great Commission is to make disciples, not to entertain Christians. Our passion should be to raise up a generation of students who will finish strong. Discipleship is not an option. Discipleship is not a program. Discipleship must become a lifestyle. It is not a ministry that we have a choice about. Yes, there are many different approaches we can take, but if we are not actively building the lives of students, we are in disobedience to God's Word.

I remember the first person I ever attempted to disciple. I was a freshman at Northwest College. One day, a very concerned mom called me at home. Her junior-high son was a rebel. She asked if I could do anything with him. To be honest, I had no idea what to do. So he and I just started to hang out together every week. We would go to the park and talk. We would discuss life and answer questions. Over the years, this young man became a strong disciple of Christ. Today, Brian Dolleman is a great youth pastor in Issaquah, Washington. I didn't disciple Brian because of a program, but out of a relationship.

There are some great discipleship programs available. To be honest with you, until discipleship becomes your passion, no program will ever help you. If discipleship is in your heart, a bad program will just temporarily set you back. Therefore, I will discuss principles that can be applied to any program. These principle are not just some theory. They are principles learned over the years. Believe me, I have attempted every type of discipleship method that you can imagine.

The greatest strength of our youth ministry was our Tuesday night discipleship program. The joy of being a youth pastor was not found in the large crowds on Wednesday nights, nor was it found in reaching six hundred students on a Friday night. The sign of accomplishment was seeing over eighty students on Tuesday nights learning how to become more like Jesus.

FIVE MISTAKES

In over ten years of youth ministry, I made some key mistakes in the area of discipleship. The reason we had an effective discipleship ministry is because I was willing to learn from these mistakes and, more importantly, I had a passion for discipleship. Let me emphasize again, if your heart beats for discipleship, no honest mistake or weak program will greatly impact your ability to disciple students. However, if you can avoid some of the most common mistakes, you will save yourself years of stress and wasted hours.

Mistake 1: Discipling Students in a Thirteen-Week Program

It is impossible to disciple students in just thirteen weeks. It cannot be done. Yes, you can get the process started, but discipleship is a lifestyle. We must teach the students that discipleship will take the rest of their lives. We must encourage them to make a commitment to three phases of discipleship, covering a fifteen-month time frame. Many students will go beyond this and even help as student leaders.

Mistake 2: Having Expectations That Don't Relate to Real Life

We must have high expectations. Students are motivated by a challenge. However, the standards must relate to real life. Every expectation must be something they can and should do for the rest of their lives. Jesus had high standards for His disciples, which He expected them to strive for when He was with them and when He went to heaven.

We also must lead by example. Every expectation you put on your students you must be doing. If you don't lead by example, your discipleship will be shallow. We reproduce who we are, not what we say.

Mistake 3: Too Much Information, Too Little Application

It is a mistake to simply offer information to your discipleship groups. Most of the time when people are looking at a particular discipleship program they are looking for teaching material, but students need to learn how to *apply* the Word. The information they receive should come from their own personal devotional time, taking notes on sermons, personally listening to the voice of God, reading good books, and memorizing Scripture. In appendix F, I provide you with a schedule that shows step by step how we actually did this.

Mistake 4: Picking Unripe Fruit

Some students are simply not ready to be involved with discipleship. We cannot force students to grow. In no way am I implying that we should give up on these students. I'd like every student to be involved with a small group.

When I first met with Brian Dolleman, he wasn't ready for an intense discipleship time. However, because of our relationship, he eventually desired this kind of influence on his life. The only way to find out if a student is ready for intense discipleship is through spending one-on-one time with him or her.

Mistake 5: Not Discipling Students

Many youth pastors and leaders make the mistake of not discipling students. There was a time in my ministry that I did not emphasize discipleship, because we tried program after program and frustration began to set in. One day I realized that even though there were definite elements I would change, those attempts I made actually impacted students' lives. The reason I am writing this book is to communicate the nuts and bolts of discipleship, so youth pastors and leaders can avoid these mistakes. Don't make the biggest mistake of all and give up. Not only will you disobey the Great Commission, but youth ministry will become very frustrating for you.

THE NUTS AND BOLTS OF DISCIPLESHIP

Develop Definite Seasons for Discipleship

I have found that the best times to do discipleship are during the fall and spring. Summer provides for some great times for discipleship at camps, on missions trips, and choir tours. Winter is difficult because of the holidays. The benefit to developing definite times for discipleship is that the students begin to look forward to it. I also like the fall and spring because these are right after our summer camps and winter retreats.

124

Our fall discipleship program started the last Tuesday of August. It is important to be totally done with this thirteen-week phase before Thanksgiving. If you can't get done by Thanksgiving, simply make it an eleven- or twelve-week time commitment. I have learned from experience not to compete with the holidays.

The spring discipleship ministry started the second Tuesday of February. One could begin a little later or even sooner, but it is important to finish this phase by the end of May, preferably before Memorial Day weekend. The important issue is to carve out times for discipleship.

Learn the Art of Leading Discipleship Groups

We must become experts in leading discipleship groups. Unfortunately, it's an art, not a science. I encourage every youth pastor and leader to watch someone who is experienced in leading these groups.

In appendix F, I have enclosed an example of one of our Tuesday night discipleship times. Over the years, I have learned the art of leading small groups of this nature. To be blunt, my wife, Jana, has taught me more than any other person about discipleship groups. Here are a couple of insights:

- *Be flexible at all times.* Listen to the voice of God and the needs of the students. Learn to flow with God.
- *Leadership is everything.* The leader must lead. We must have wisdom in not allowing distractions or one student to dominate. We must love the students and bring out the best in each one.
- *The most important time is before, after, and during the week.* We must be available to love and listen to the students during those times. One reason a discipleship group should end on time is so refreshments can be provided and the students and leader can simply hang out together.

- *Give opportunity for reflection and input.* Keep asking the students questions, such as, "What is God teaching you during your prayer times?" or, "What did you learn during Bible reading this week?" or, "How have you applied last week's sermon?"
- *Give opportunity for worship and prayer time.* This may take up the whole agenda. As long as it is effective, don't be overly concerned.
- *Give opportunity for gifts of the Spirit.* Students need to see and learn how to operate in the gifts.
- *Begin and end on time.*

Environment Is Vital

The environment of your discipleship group is vitally important, and it ultimately hinges on the relationships within the group. We need to give the students a platform on which to build these relationships. The first time they may not click together. However, you must find creative ways to build these relationships among the group. Students who play together pray together. Do something fun together, even before the first official meeting.

The following are some environmental issues:

- *Location.* I have found that the best location for a discipleship group is in a home. I realize there are some definite challenges to this. However, I would do everything possible to provide the home environment.
- *Day to meet.* This all depends on the calendar and weekly schedule of you and your students. I did Tuesday evenings because Sunday afternoons were for leadership meetings and Monday, Thursday, and Saturdays were my family nights. Perhaps you could consider a time after school or a Saturday morning. No matter when you decide to meet, someone will not be able to come. Just decide on a time and be consistent.

- *The size of the group is important but not crucial.* I prefer to keep the groups between twelve and fifteen students. However, depending on the leader, some groups just naturally get bigger than that. If I don't have another leader ready to go, I will let that group grow until we are ready to add a new group.
- *If possible, keep the groups composed of the same gender.*

Encourage All Three Phases of Discipleship

Remember, discipleship can't happen in thirteen weeks; discipleship is a lifestyle. Encourage the students to go through three phases of discipleship, but require them only to commit to one phase at a time. The goal is to have every student in your youth ministry commit fifteen months of their teenage lives to a specific discipleship group and have them commit the rest of their lives to the discipleship mandate.

For example, if a student begins fall discipleship in September 1998, he/she won't be totally completed until November 1999. In real life, some students may skip a phase or even decide not to go on; but don't let this discourage you. And don't limit a student to three phases of discipleship. Some may want to do four or five phases, and others may want to be a student leader in discipleship.

The following are the benefits to having students go through three phases of discipleship:

- *After the phases are completed, the students begin to develop a discipleship lifestyle.*
- *The students have discipline and accountably for fifteen months.* Even though there are breaks in the program, I emphasize that there is never a break in discipleship.
- *The students have a chance to disciple new students who join.* It is very important that you don't endeavor to keep the same group together for the fifteen-month period. This is a common mistake that creates an inward focus in the

students. Also, it is unrealistic to think all the students will undertake the fifteen-month commitment at one stretch. By involving new students at the beginning of a particular phase, they have a chance to disciple each other and it keeps new life in the program. Discipleship that is based upon application and not solely on more information makes it possible to incorporate new students all the time. But involve new students only at the beginning of each phase.

Prepare Students Months before You Begin

One of the greatest mistakes we make in discipleship is that we don't prepare students for the commitment they are about to make. We simply mention it to them and have them fill out an application. We must cast the vision personally to the student, months before the actual day begins. This will greatly impact the way the students walk in on the first day.

- *Cast the vision with enthusiasm.* Vision motivates action in the hearts of students. Let them know they are about to do one of the greatest ministries of their life. Don't apologize for the high standards and for the fact they may have to give up sports or some other type of activity.
- *Speak life into the students one on one.* Get them alone after the service or at a local restaurant and let them know you are proud of them for the commitment they are about to make.
- *Talk to them privately.* During your summer camps and retreats, God is working in their hearts. Students want to know what is the next step. Let them know the next step begins in the fall with discipleship.
- *Pray for students who commit to discipleship.* The first Wednesday after we started discipleship, I would bring all the students forward and pray for them. This prepared students for the next phase of discipleship.

Build on the Word

If we don't teach our students to love and have a passion for the Word, they will simply be gone with the wind. They need to learn how to personally read, study, memorize, and apply the Word of God. The goal of discipleship is not to have another Bible study or more information; it's to teach them to reflect on and apply the Word.

One of the main characteristics of infants is they need someone else to feed them. Yet, discipleship is not you feeding the students, but teaching them to feed themselves on the Word. The following are some insights on building a discipleship ministry on the Word:

- *Teach how-to versus ought-to lessons.* We need to teach our students how to pray, how to grow, how to read the Bible, etc. In appendix F, I give you a list of twenty-one how-to lessons—seven lessons for each phase of discipleship. I have found this is more than enough for thirteen weeks. Keep the lessons short and very practical in nature.
- *Provide a one-year Bible reading plan.* Instead of having a plan just for the thirteen weeks, provide one that students can follow all year.
- *Discuss the Word.* I have already mentioned the need to ask the students what they are learning while reading the Bible. This puts a value on their reading time.
- *Have them take notes while reading the Bible.*
- *Memorize Scripture together.* Assign at least one verse a week. By the end of one phase, every student should have at least ten scriptures totally memorized.

Provide a Notebook Students Can Use Their Whole Lives

Too many times we provide the students with so much paperwork they barely read it all, let alone use it outside of the group. We need to follow the KISS principle (Keep it simple, stupid) when it comes to discipleship. The following is a list of the five notebook sections I gave to the students that became a tool they could use in other areas. All the students needed was this notebook and their Bible and they were ready for discipleship. The five section names and contents include:

1. *Prayer*: a prayer list and blank sheets to record answered prayers
2. *Bible*: including a Bible reading plan, Scripture memorization record, and blank sheets to take notes
3. *Reflection*: blank sheets to use as a journal
4. *Sermon notes*: some blank sheets for notes on all sermons and Tuesday night teaching for fifteen months
5. *Planning*: including discipleship requirements; thirteen accountability sheets; and the dates for discipleship meetings, retreats, and any other events

Establish Accountability

We must establish a process to keep the students accountable to the requirements. The requirements need to be high and relate to real life outside of the program. For example, to forbid TV is not realistic for the rest of their lives. My guideline was to allow only five hours a week of TV that Jesus would watch. That is more than reasonable as an expectation for the rest of their lives. Have the requirements in writing. Appendix G has a list of the ones I used.

- *In detail and with no apology, cover the requirements the first day of discipleship.*
- *Have every student turn in an accountability sheet each week.* Appendix H has an example of an accountability sheet. The first thing the students should do when they arrive for discipleship is to turn these in to you. If they don't have them done, have them fill one out right away, before you begin. It is very important that you give feedback and return these to the students within twenty-four hours. With a red pen, circle areas of concern, and then always make a positive comment on the bottom. Let them know you love and

believe in them. Perhaps you could return those sheets to the students at church the next day or send them in the mail. Your comments will make a world of difference.

End Each Phase with a Retreat

Perhaps some of the greatest times we had were during our discipleship retreats twice a year. These were times of intense prayer and celebration of growth. The only way students could go on these retreats was to have successfully completed a particular phase of discipleship. And the students paid for each one-night retreat.

Add; Don't Divide

Many people make the mistake of growing a discipleship group to a particular size and then dividing it. This sounds good in theory but never really works. Hold groups only during the fall and spring to deal with the size challenge. The groups must not become focused inwardly; the leader sets the right attitude.

The way to successfully grow your discipleship ministry is to simply add new groups at the beginning of a phase. This is the perfect opportunity to encourage students to think about joining a new group. Adding new discipleship groups removes the awkwardness of dividing relationships in the middle of a phase.

Be careful; don't add new groups without effective leadership. I would rather have a group that's too big than one led with ineffective leadership. Add slowly and with much wisdom. It took me years to develop five home discipleship groups on Tuesday nights. When adding a new discipleship group, keep these insights in mind:

- *Involve students from other discipleship groups.*
- *Make sure you have an effective leader.*
- *Use your best leader to pioneer a new group.* For example, when my wife's group got too big (over forty) she started a new one just for junior high and allowed the two other leaders to begin their own.

Chapter Sixteen

Camp Survival Kit

—◦«◉»◦—

Without Bible camps, our churches would be void
of leadership within one decade.
—*Troy Jones*

One of the greatest ways we can build students is through camps
and retreats. Something happens in the heart of a student when
he or she can retreat from everyting and begin to let God work in
his or her life. More students are saved, baptized in the Holy Spirit,
and called into ministry at retreats and camps than at any of the
other ministries churches do. Something happens in the heart of a
student when he or she can retreat from everything and begin to
let God work in his or her life.

There is no doubt that my deep belief in camps and retreats is
influenced by the fact I was saved at Cedar Springs camp. God
took this broken junior-high student and in five days and four
nights totally turned my life around.

At a five-day camp we spend sixty-two waking hours with students. We spend more time with them in one week than we do all
year, even if they faithfully attend our youth services. In this environment, relationships are built and God is able to make a perma-
nent mark on students' lives.

The following are five decisions we need to make in developing a successful camp:

Decision 1: Decide the "Why" behind the Event

There are many different types of camps, but I will deal specifically with camps that are designed to *build* students for Christ. This in no way implies that students don't get saved at "build" camps. I was saved at a camp with this focus. I understand the power of seeing students get saved at every camp/retreat we do.

If you want to hold a camp or retreat to build and encourage students, you must strategically think through every service. For example, a weekend retreat might have only an evening service because a handful of kids will want to go skiing during the morning hours. Take them skiing some other time, and hold a service in the morning. It is unfortunate how much time we waste when we are not focused on impacting students for eternity.

FOUR ELEMENTS OF A BUILD CAMP

- *The Word*: When you get together for a week or weekend, it's a great opportunity to teach your students to read the Bible daily. At every camp, retreat, missions trip, and youth choir tour, we were always reading a book of the Bible.
- *Worship*: Don't compromise in this area. We must train our students to worship. If you have to bring someone in for this, do it.
- *Altar*: Don't allow anything to hinder your altar times. Be careful what you plan for late-night events. The students must know that anything that gets in the way of the altar has second priority.
- *Relationships*: This is where some free time and scheduled activities are very healthy. Your staff must understand that their role is essential at this point. They need to spend their time loving and hanging out with the students.

Decision 2: Decide the Budget

Learn to underestimate your income and to overestimate your expenses. Become an expert in the area of budgeting. A budget crisis can ruin the effect of a camp more quickly than anything.

Here are some budget items to think about:

- Facility
- Food and snacks
- Speaker
- Worship leader
- Gas and transportation
- Leaders' expenses
- Sports and prizes
- Unexpected expenses

MONEY-SAVING IDEAS

- *Provide your own food.* Not every facility allows for this, but we found some facilities did. Parents love to come and do the cooking. We saved big dollars in this way.
- *Have a local speaker.* This doesn't save money on the honorarium, but it does save travel expenses.
- *Brainstorm about the facility.* We were able to find environment-training facilities for a very reasonable rate. Other ideas are churches, tent sites, etc.
- *Don't give out full scholarships.* It took me years to learn this lesson. Giving out full scholarships is not good for the students, and it costs you money.
- *Take offerings.* Here are four possible times you can take offerings to help underwrite your camps:

  1. Midweek service prior to camp
  2. During camp, for the speaker
  3. Sunday evening/final service at home church
  4. Sunday morning to help with scholarships

- *Charge leaders half price.* This generates a positive response because it shows gratitude toward leaders and keeps the price down on the retreat.

Decision 3: Decide the "When" for the Event

Retreats and camps need to be strategically planned. The following are six times a year we held our camps and retreats:

1. *January*: This is when we did our winter retreat, an all-youth event enabling the students to wait on God.
2. *May*: In May we did our spring discipleship retreat. This was an effective way to conclude the discipleship phase.
3. *July/August*: During the summer we cooperated with our district's Bible camps.
4. *September*: This retreat is for all leaders to plan and dream together for the fall.
5. *October*: The fall youth convention was a highlight for our students to get together with thousands of others to celebrate the power of God and prepare to reach their campuses for Christ.
6. *November*: We held the discipleship retreat, which concluded our fall discipleship.

I believe that we all need times set aside in order to retreat with God. It never ceases to amaze me what God can do even overnight when we get away from all distractions and let Him move.

Decision 4: Choose the Speaker

The most important person at your camp/retreat is the speaker. Occasionally, I hear leaders comment, "I don't want to build around the speaker." I totally disagree with this statement. I want another voice to speak into the lives of my students. I want to bring a speaker in who will influence my students in a way I can't.

As a youth pastor, I identified key individuals I wanted to influence my students. Instead of bringing in a lot of speakers, I strategically handpicked a select few, who joined hands with me to pastor my youth. This allowed the students to build relationships with the speakers. Also, it made it easier to communicate excitement about the event at any given time. Here are a few practical ideas I used:

- *Bring the speaker in to speak three months before the retreat.* This helps motivate the students to attend the event.
- *Bring the speaker back within a month after the retreat.* This can be a great outreach if the speaker is gifted.
- *Have the speaker return, preaching two years in a row at the retreat.* Obviously we must be careful not to overuse a speaker, but there are many benefits to bringing a speaker back for a second year. In more than ten years of planning winter retreats, I had to find only five speakers whom I trusted.

PAYING THE SPEAKER

We must be generous with our speakers. At times we spend more money on the gas to get to the facility than we do on our speaker. How we spend our money shows where we place value. It is a tragedy if we spend more on our breakfast than what we give to our speaker. This shows that we value natural food more than spiritual food.

The following are insights on paying a speaker:

1. *Pay all expenses.* Don't let him or her pay for anything. This includes:

   - Travel/mileage expenses (32.5¢ per mile)
   - Spouse's expenses
   - All food, including snacks/drinks
   - Phone expenses

2. *Give a generous honorarium immediately after the event.* There are so many variables on what you should pay a speaker.

The following are four questions one needs to think about when paying a speaker.

A. *What kind of experience does he or she have?* The more experience and longevity, the more generous the honorarium should be.
B. *How many students will be there?* The more students, the more the honorarium should be.
C. *Did the speaker's name help advertising?* If the speaker's name was the draw, he or she should benefit from this.
D. *Is this the speaker's sole means of support?* If so, you need to realize that you're not only paying their weekly check, but you're also paying for their vacation time, insurance, office supplies, other employees, Social Security, Christmas bonus, etc.

I wouldn't expect any speaker to come for a two-night retreat for less than $500. This may sound like a lot of money; however, there are three ways I received the income to pay for this:

- *Students' registration.* Budget a percentage of each registration fee to go to the speaker.
- *Offerings at camp.* This gives the students a chance to bless the speaker.
- *Offerings at the Sunday evening service.* I invited our speaker to conclude our retreats at the Sunday evening service at the church. This would be a great time for the church to see what God did at the retreat. Also, it gave me a platform to take an offering for the speaker.

One final note, there are a lot of little things you can do that go beyond any amount of money you give. Brainstorm with your staff on ideas. Be creative! Here are a few ideas:

- *Fruit/breakfast basket sent to the speaker's room.*
- *Take time to personally say thank you.*

- *Arrange good sleeping accommodations.* If he or she needs a sleeping bag, provide one.
- *Do not waste the speaker's time.* For example, if your final service is a quick one, where you really don't need the speaker, send him or her home to be with family.
- *Pay the speaker before he or she leaves.* It is inappropriate to send the speaker a check. Plan ahead so you are prepared to pay at the conclusion of the event.
- *Give the speaker good references.*
- *Send him/her directions and any other helpful information.*
- *Arrange all the accommodations, even if he or she wants to bring a spouse and children.*

Decision 5: Decide the Schedule

See appendix I for an example of a weekend retreat. While many variables must be considered, this will help in your planning. Also, see appendix J for a worksheet on planning a retreat in a year. Let me highlight a couple of key ideas that significantly assisted our schedule.

- *Hold an orientation before you leave the church.* This allows you to get right into your service at the camp. Also, it gets people on the same page before you leave.
- *At least one year in advance, nail down the date, speaker, and facility.*
- *If possible, end the retreat in your home church.* This helps with finances and church support.
- *Have students bring money for one or two meals.* Schedule stops for food on the way to and/or from the retreat.
- *Don't waste mornings.* This is a great time to train students in leadership, daily prayer, campus ministry, finances, etc.
- *Print out a simple schedule for all students and leaders.* Be flexible. I have never seen a camp/retreat schedule that was followed to the letter.

SECTION FOUR
SEND

INTRODUCTION

S *ending* is perhaps the most significant aspect for building an effective youth ministry. If students don't use their gifts for God, they will become apathetic and critical. Go to any sporting event. The most negative and unsupportive people are those sitting in the bleachers. We must become experts at mobilizing people to get into the game.

Again, according to Ephesians 4:12–13, my main responsibility as a pastor is to equip God's people for works of service. Yet so many of us pride ourselves in the long hours we put in—spending most of our time doing the ministry and complaining that nobody wants to help. We need to take all of the wasted time doing and complaining and begin to release God's people into ministry. If we don't learn this principle, we will kill ourselves, destroy our families, hinder God's church, and hinder the growth of the people we are ministering to.

You must *release* ministry more than you *do* ministry. This was the principle God taught the early church (see Acts 6). The immediate result was church growth.

CHAPTER SEVENTEEN

DEVELOPING UNLIMITED LEADERS

———◦((◦))◦———

You can buy a man's time, you can even buy his physical
presence at a given place, but you cannot buy
Enthusiasms . . . you cannot buy Loyalty . . . you cannot buy
the devotion of one's heart, soul, or mind.
You must earn these.

—Charles Frances

The key to reaching the students of the twenty-first century is
to develop adults who will believe and invest time in them.
You will never grow a youth ministries beyond your ability to grow
a leadership team around it. This is why so many ministries have
been the same size for years.

Students are plentiful and ready to be reached. Jesus taught us
this principle in Matthew 9:37–38 when he said, "The harvest is
plentiful but the workers are few. Ask the Lord of the harvest, therefore, to send out workers into his harvest." Notice that Jesus did not
say to ask for more souls. Jesus knew souls would come automati-
cally when the leaders showed up. We need to pray daily that God
would give us unlimited leaders.

Over the years, I developed over 110 people on my leadership
team. In the process I have learned some key principles that work.

Using the acronym UNLIMITED, here are some insights on developing unlimited leaders in your church.

Unleash Growth in Your Life

We talked about growth in section 1. It would be worth your time to review that section again and again. The bottom line to building a big youth ministry is building a big *you*. You will never recruit a bigger leader than you are. Many of us simply can't recruit leaders beyond some leftovers at the church, because the people in our churches are bigger leaders than we are. This may be a difficult pill to swallow, but why should some guy who is the CEO of his company work for you when you can't even be on time to the office? Why should that busy mother give her time to your ministry when she organizes her towels better than you organize a retreat?

We must have a hunger to grow. Be willing to hang out with people who are doing ministry better than you are. Listen to tapes. Read some leadership books.

Nonstoppable Structure

We need to create a structure that involves everyone. When we take a nonstop flight somewhere, it means there are no layovers. We also must get rid of all the layovers—limits—we put on people. My goal was to involve someone in my youth ministry if he/she could give one hour a day to one hour a week. Many youth pastors don't have unlimited leaders, because they have way too many limits on who they will involve. I remember going to one conference where the speaker had so many qualifications for his leaders that very few would ever measure up. Then he proudly said he only had six people who met all of those qualities. Jesus would have had a difficult time working on his staff.

Yes, we need to have high standards; however, don't wait for people to walk on water before you let them wait on tables. In appendix K there is a list of requirements for youth staff. One of the common mistakes youth pastors and leaders make is having a list of requirements that nobody, including themselves, can even remember. We need to be flexible as long as it relates to the time we require of people.

THE PEOPLE IN A NONSTOPPABLE STRUCTURE

- *Youth staff*: These were adults and leaders who did one-on-one ministry for the students. I trained them on the second and fourth Sundays of the month. All of my interns—junior high, senior high, etc.—and any other ministry leader were on youth staff.
- *Y-SIT (youth staff in training)*: These were seniors in high school who attended our training meeting while being prepared for youth staff in the future.
- *Support workers*: These were adults who provided an incredible support. I would have died without these workers. I met with them only once a year for a time of appreciation, but I communicated often by letters and phone. Some of these adults gave one main commitment a year; others gave weekly commitments. These adults included parents, senior citizens, young couples, single parents, and experts.
- *Student leaders*: These were students who provided unlimited energy and work for the youth ministry. I trained them on the first Sunday of each month. Many of these student leaders were also campus missionaries.
- *Informal leadership*: This was anybody and everybody I could involve in ministry. If I saw a parent after an event, I would ask him or her to jump in. Even a heathen can move chairs. Open up your mind to the possibilities. To quote Tommy Barnett, "The miracle is in the house."

Longevity Builds Leadership Around You

One main reason I had so many leaders and people willing to help out is because I was at Renton Assembly for eighteen years.

People will jump in when there is a relationship and trust. If you can't make a commitment to be faithful to a church, why should others make a commitment to your ministry? Enough said. Read section 1 again to review that information. Appendix L has a leadership application you can use for the areas of ministry you have available.

Involve Everybody Every Time and Everywhere

We must make it our business to involve everybody in our youth ministry. The only exception is to never involve anyone with a history of child molestation. Also, be careful to use unbelievers behind the scenes only. The following is a list of some of the most common people we don't involve but who could greatly benefit us:

- People who don't attend our church
- Parents of youth
- New believers
- People we have to pay/experts
- Senior citizens
- Busy people
- People new to the church
- Young couples with kids
- Students
- People who don't walk on water
- Other staff at the church

If not these people, then whom? The reason we don't have unlimited people involved is we don't involve some obvious candidates right in front of us. If you do ministry alone, you deserve to do ministry alone. One reason Jesus has us to do ministry in twos is to multiply ourselves.

Every time includes the following days:

- Sunday
- Monday
- Tuesday

- Wednesday
- Thursday
- Friday
- Saturday

Involving people in ministry *everywhere* is when youth pastors and leaders make their greatest mistake. We lose more potential help in our ministries simply because we don't know where to involve them. At times, we are so busy we don't stop and meet the person to find out where they are gifted. If any potential leader showed up at a Wednesday night service, I invited them out to eat immediately after the service. My wife knew that on any given Wednesday night or Sunday night after church we would go out with a potential leader.

Winners don't want to sit around and watch you minister. I have learned through much trial and error that either you *use* people, or you will *lose* people. Most people are asking the wrong question, "How do I get more leaders?" Begin to ask, "Where will I use the leaders once they come?" The following two lists will help you begin to think through these questions.

COMMON RESPONSIBILITIES FOR YOUTH STAFF
- Fellowship groups
- Calling students
- Organizing events
- Friday Nite Hangout staff
- Sunday school teachers
- Staff at camps and retreats

COMMON RESPONSIBILITIES FOR SUPPORT STAFF
- Taking roll on Sunday morning
- Counting offering on Wednesday night
- Giving out nametags on Wednesday night
- Senior citizens praying for two specific students a year
- Driving buses and vans
- Picking up students in cars

- Helping with mailers and secretarial work
- Helping in the café at FNH
- Signing in students at FNH
- Fundraisers
- Sponsoring snak-n-yaks at homes
- Cooking at winter retreats

Motivate through Vision

Vision motivates people into action. Believe me, if there's fire in your life, people will come and watch you burn. We attempt to motivate people in many ineffective ways.

FOUR MOTIVATION METHODS THAT DON'T WORK
1. Badgering people
2. Begging people
3. Boring people with dry programs
4. Bulletin approach

Those may work for awhile. However, the only way to truly motivate people is with vision. If you have a big dream, you will have unlimited leaders. Some of us need only five leaders, because that is how big our dream is.

HOW TO CAST VISION
- *Give a State-of-the-Youth-Ministry address every year.* I stood before our church every year and cast the vision for our youth ministry. The church allowed me to do this the second Sunday of every February. Before I gave this address, I cast the vision to the leadership team and youth ministry as a whole. More leaders joined our youth ministry in February than any other time of the year because of this vision casting. In my address, I never once cried that nobody wanted to help out.

- *Cast the vision every thirty days.* People will forget the vision very easily. It is our responsibility to be creative in the way we communicate the vision to our students and church.
- *Speak the vision one on one.* Learn to talk about the vision God has placed on your heart. Get together with students and leaders often and share the vision.
- *Write the vision down.* This will help you clarify your thoughts. Give the vision to your people to pray over. Have enough courage to print and pass the vision out. As I stated earlier in the book, your vision needs to be simple enough to explain to a child in thirty seconds or less. Also, you need to develop a chart that people can use for tracking your vision. The chart that I have built this book around is an excellent resource.

Invest in Future Pastors

We have a responsibility to reproduce ourselves. I strongly believe that all ministers should have young adults under them who they are training for full-time ministry. I am tired of hearing youth pastors and leaders complain about our Bible colleges. Stop complaining, join hands with the institutes, and together we can make a difference.

At Renton Assembly I trained and released twelve youth pastors into full-time ministry. These youth pastors were exposed to an effective youth ministry while getting their Bible education at Northwest College or some other school.

HOW TO INVEST IN FUTURE PASTORS
- *Plant seeds into students.* We need to encourage students to consider the fact that God could be calling them into full-time ministry. While we must be careful not to tell someone that they are called, it is our responsibility to challenge them to search their hearts for the call of God.
- *Be committed to the education-and-experience approach.* I believe the only way to train a future pastor is by providing

him or her with a quality education and hands-on experience. Any program that compromises in either of these areas is shortchanging the student. This is why I have a big problem with some Master's Commission programs and why we started an MIT (Ministers in training) program. In essence, this requires the students to attend Bible college while giving them fifteen hours of experience per week at a local church.

- *Celebrate when someone is sent out.* Perhaps some of the greatest youth services we had were when we sent out a new youth pastor. We would pray and anoint them with oil, and we would take an offering for them and let them know we loved and believed in their ministry.

- *Set aside time in your calendar.* My calendar had definite times set aside to just hang out with future pastors. Every Wednesday, I would meet with MIT students and give them encouragement and training.

The greatest and most fulfilling ministry I have ever been involved with is training future pastors. Besides leading someone to Jesus for the first time, there is no greater joy or excitement.

Train and Equip Leaders

Every ministry that failed under my leadership can be traced back to this one thing: I did not train the leader. So many of us are guilty of simply putting people into leadership without any type of training. We must come up with a solid and consistent way to train our leadership. Let me give you three guidelines that helped:

1. *Train by walking around.* On Sunday morning, my responsibility was to walk around and encourage my students and youth staff. When I saw something that needed help, I would train the leader in a very positive way later on that week.
2. *Train through special seminars.* Take your leaders with you to leadership seminars.

3. *Train at youth staff meetings.* At our meetings, I would spend time training and equipping. Our leaders received information that was very beneficial to their whole lives. Here is a schedule of a typical youth staff meeting:

- Opening worship and prayer   10 min.
- Practical leadership training   20 min.
- Refreshment break   5 min.
- Ministry/Communication   25 min.
- Group staff meetings   25 min. (These were meetings in which the junior high, senior high, and choir youth staff would meet.)

4. *Train with practical leadership lessons.* Make your staff meetings beneficial to the leaders. Train them in ares of leadership that will help them be a better person. Here are some subjects I would cover:

- Financial health
- How to keep growing
- Dealing with conflict—problem solving
- How to motivate people
- Convictions about ministry
- How to win, build, and send students
- Spiritual gifts
- Impacting the local campus
- Personal ethics

Encourage People

The way to draw people to your ministry is through encouragement. Hebrews 3:13 says we need to encourage people daily so their hearts will remain soft. The ironic thing is that we spend our time begging people to get involved; yet, if we would just encourage everybody, we would have unlimited workers. Three principles that guide my leadership style are:

1. *Give people a raise by praise.* The greatest way to give someone a raise is by telling them you appreciate their work. At times, this is more valuable than a paycheck. A thank-you letter or word of encouragement goes a long way.
2. *Catch people in the act of doing good.* We tend to talk to people only when there is a problem. That is a mistake. When a leader does something you like, say so.
3. *No public begging; only public bragging.* In more than a decade of youth ministry, I never once from the pulpit asked for help. All I did was mention how much I appreciated one of my leaders and that without him there would be no ministry. This drew in unlimited leaders.

Decide to Never Do Ministry Alone

I was at one of John Maxwell's conferences when I learned this principle. He spent an incredible amount of time saying there were four words that grew his ministry; four words that will change our lives and guarantee significance in ministry. The four words were *Never do ministry alone.*

The word *never* includes:

- Never visit a student alone
- Never go to a campus alone
- Never go to the hospital alone
- Never go to lunch alone
- Never teach a class alone

CHAPTER EIGHTEEN

GETTING STUDENTS OFF THE BENCH

Never learn to do anything. If you don't learn, you will
always find someone else to do it for you.
—*Mark Twain*

One of the main reasons students become bored with church is because they are not created by God to watch the pastor blab each week. We must release students into ministry. One of the main differences between a youth group and a youth ministry is that one *watches* the leader minister, and the other strategically *releases* students into ministry.

As youth pastors and leaders, we have the greatest work force in the church. There should never be a reason to complain about a lack of help. No other ministry at your church has this automatic work force built in. My vision was for every ministry in the church to look to the youth ministry for needed help.

It is totally unbiblical for a pastor to do everything. Students are incredibly gifted by God, so we must provide a platform for them to use their gifts. I personally feel I am stealing from the students' potential if I do everything.

THE YOUTH PASTOR OR LEADER AS A COACH

We need to view ourselves as coaches. I am going to use the analogy of a coach to help us see what our responsibility as pastors should be. Imagine a coach leading his team the way we lead our youth ministries: A couple of times a week he would gather with them and give them the plays and instruct them to not lose the passion for the game. That would be a losing team. Why? Unless the team actually grabs the football during practice and knows they will be playing soon, there will very little motivation.

There are many characteristics of a good coach. The following are five that will directly change the way you do youth ministry.

A Coach Trains More Than He Teaches

PRINCIPLE: *Students will line up to be involved in ministry if the leader provides effective training.*

There is a big difference between *training* and *teaching*. Training is showing people how to live the information, and teaching is imparting information. A coach would be ineffective if all he did was give the history of the game, expound on some thoughts about it, and end with a challenge for the team. He would be fired.

The following are ways to train students:

- *Train them to see their campuses as playing fields and your service as the locker room.*
- *Train them to pray at a weekly prayer meeting.* We learn how to pray by praying, just like we learn how to play football by playing football. I believe every youth pastor or leader should be the first one to pray in their weekly prayer meetings.
- *Train them by scheduling unlimited opportunities to minister.* We need to look for creative new ways to involve students in the game.
- *Train them in a monthly meeting.* The first Sunday of every month was our student leadership meeting. We ran this with exactly the same format as the youth staff meetings.

A Coach Builds More Than He Belittles

PRINCIPLE: *Students will line up to be involved in ministry if the leader encourages and believes in them.*

I realize not all coaches build and speak life into their team. However, a great coach knows how to build his players and bring out the best in each and every player. During games, he is there to celebrate victories and give encouragement during losses. He pushes the team players to excellence without demoralizing them. We must become experts in building and encouraging our students.

Here are some tips on building team players:

- *Speak life into them individually.* Look students right in the eyes and let them know you believe in them. So many students hear only negative talk at home and even in church. Be a coach who speaks life right into their spirits.
- *Sit by them at church.* I realize this is not always possible. However, when it is possible, go out of your way to sit by a particular student. When I asked a group of our key students what brought them to our youth ministry, one young lady shared that she came for a number of Wednesdays and nobody sat by her. She explained that she came back one more time to see if anyone would give her the time of day. Jana, my wife, sat by her that night. This young lady said she was serving God because of that.
- *Show up on their campuses.* The campus is their mission field. When you show up, it's like a coach standing on the football field, cheering the player on.
- *Recognize them publicly.* One Wednesday night during my preaching, I had a young lady stand. I prayed that God would use her on her campus. That simple prayer changed the life of that junior-high student. She became an active "player" on her campus.
- *Notes of encouragement.* A note from a youth pastor or leader can change the life of a student forever.

There are many ways to build team players. Hebrews 10:24 says we should consider how to provoke one another on to love and good deeds.

A Coach Schedules More Than He Spits

PRINCIPLE: *Students will line up to be involved in ministry if the leader schedules unlimited opportunities.*

A coach has two basic responsibilities: to schedule practice times and to communicate the times of the games. I realize this is in simple terms, but if a coach doesn't do these two basic things, there will be no team. It is the people in the bleachers who have the most negative attitudes during games. We must stop talking and spitting about it and begin to carve out times on our schedules.

Here are some of the many ways we can involve our students in ministry:

- *See the ministry menu on Youth Pastors Web Site* (www.nwdyouth.com). On our Web site, I have provided you with a menu that offers a variety of ministry opportunities.
- *Student leadership.* We depended on student leaders for almost everything. They helped set up Friday Nite Hangout, make calls, follow up on new people, set up for Wednesday night, worship team—the list could go on forever. Our leadership training was the first Sunday of the month from 4:00 to 5:30 P.M.
- *All-church involvement.* It should be the goal of every youth pastor and leader to have his/her students involved in key areas of the church. The students should be the work force. I remember once coming home from a winter retreat that ended on a Sunday. It seemed that the whole church was angry with me. I didn't understand until my senior pastor explained that the following areas were not covered, because the youth group was gone: ushers, friendship registers,

Sunday school teachers, nursery workers, bus captains, over-head projectors, worship team, super church helpers, etc. We should have communicated better that we were going to be gone; but I was one proud youth pastor that day.

- *Children's ministry.* One of the greatest ways students can be involved in ministry is with the children's and nursery ministries. I encouraged them to especially be involved Sunday mornings and nights. This gave them the opportunity to be active with the youth ministry on Wednesday night.
- *New-people ministry.* Involve students in reaching out to new people. They can do that by calling them, greeting them at the door, helping with recognizing them in the service, or visiting them at home.
- *Ask other "coaches."* There are many excellent opportunities that exist. Make it your business to call and ask other youth pastors and leaders for ideas.

A Coach Wins More Than He Whines

PRINCIPLE: *Students will line up to be involved with ministry if the leader develops a winning team.*

No one wants to be around a losing team. It is time to develop a winning team. Why are people excited about Michael Jordan and the Bulls? Because they have won six championships. I guarantee that if the students know they will win when they get involved with ministry, there will be no stopping them.

The greatest way to kill the morale of a team is to have a *whining* attitude. Too many youth pastors and leaders spend their time whining all the time, "I have no help. . . . My church doesn't support me. . . . My senior pastor doesn't give me pulpit time. . . . I have to raise all my support. . . . No one understands. . . . No one is here tonight. . . . I always have to stay late."

Stop all your whining.

Some of us need to get a real job and find out what work is all about. I don't mean to be harsh, but all that whining is the very reason why you are losing. The following are some ideas for developing a winning team:

- *Strategically place your players.* Put young people in situations that will challenge them but ones you know they can be successful in.
- *Establish a no-whining rule.* If done correctly, it will change the life of your ministry. I don't allow specific words in my ministry, such as: *shut up, boring, stupid, nobody is here,* etc. I told my young people those words were like cussing.
- *Celebrate your wins.* Learn to celebrate every victory you have. At your services, shout and make it a big deal if someone got saved, if you gave $1,000 to missions, if the prayer meeting was powerful, etc.
- *Have a game plan.* A good coach and everybody on the team know the game plan. As stated in chapter 1, a youth pastors with significance will:

  1. Know their purpose
  2. Show their plan
  3. Grow their people
  4. Flow with their problems

Every youth pastor and leader should have a mission statement and specific goal. You should be able to clearly communicate how you plan to win students for Christ, build students on the Word, and send students into the world.

A Coach Asks Strategic Questions versus Simple Questions

PRINCIPLE: *Students will line up to be involved with ministry if the leader asks strategic and hard questions.*

If we ask wrong questions, we get wrong answers. A great coach is not so concerned with the outcome of the game as much as why they lose or win. Team players tend to get caught up in the emotion of the game. As a good coach, it is very important to celebrate the wins and not ignore the losses; however, we need to learn to ask "why" in every situation.

It is very shallow and ineffective to ask only how many students we have in our youth services. As a coach who is committed to involving *every* player in the game, here are some strategic questions you need to reflect on:

- What are the spiritual gifts of each of my students?
- Why was this youth service/event so successful?
- Why was this youth service/event ineffective?
- What am I doing that somebody else should be doing?
- If we stop doing this ministry, would anyone notice?

CHAPTER NINTEEN

INVEST IN THE BEST

━━━◄(◐)►━━━

Some people like to give God all the credit but not the cash.
—*Anonymous*

Students need to be involved with a ministry that is bigger than they are. They need a sense of destiny. Every youth pastor and leader needs to make it his/her priority to teach students how to tithe and give to missions.

There's a fundamental difference between a youth ministry and a youth group: A youth ministry *gives*, and a youth group *spends*. It concerns me if my group gives more to the local McDonald's than we do to our missionaries.

I firmly believe giving to missions should be a mandate of every youth ministry. And as youth pastors and leaders, we need to find a platform for our students to give to missions. One of the best I know is Speed-the-Light (STL). STL is a missions program that provides all the vehicles and equipment for Assemblies of God missionaries; and it's supported by many different denominations. Without Speed-the-Light, our missionaries' ministries would be crippled.

In your particular setting, STL may not be within the frame-work of your vision and/or denomination. I will refer to Speed-the-Light throughout this chapter; but these principles can be applied to any mission-giving endeavor. We may not give to Speed-

161

the-Light, but we all have the responsibility to teach our students to give to missions.

EIGHT STEPS TOWARD FUNDING MISSIONS

Step 1: Your Pastor Gives

We must lead by example. Every church pastor and leader should make sure they are leading by example in the area of giving. When I see a church giving $1,000, I know the leader himself is giving $1,000 or less to missions. I cannot overemphasize this principle. We must lead by example in our giving to missions.

Step 2: Your Youth Staff Gives

Giving must begin with leadership. I required all my youth staff to give to missions. Now, I didn't necessarily check up on them. It was an issue of integrity. If the leadership isn't giving, the students simply won't give. End of story. I took goals from the leaders before I took them from the students. It was a powerful motivation to the students to see the staff giving.

Step 3: Students Give

We must train our students to be givers. That will change the way our students live in every area of their lives. If we don't train our students in the area of finances, we are raising up a generation that will not experience the blessing of God.

HOW TO MOTIVATE STUDENTS TO GIVE
- *See the Youth Pastors Web Site* (www.nwdyouth.com).
- *Every year, have the students make a goal to missions giving.* If your church has a missions convention, that would be an excellent time to do faith promises with your students.
- *Send a copy of the goal cards to them once a quarter with a friendly reminder from the youth pastor.*

- *Commit the vast majority of the Sunday school and midweek offering to missions giving.* This will make a big difference. When Pastor Rick Ross agreed to allow our Sunday school offerings to be designated to missions, it made a difference. No matter how small, they all add up at the end of the year. Five dollars a week adds up to $260 a year.
- *Avoid underchallenging the students by saying things like, "Everybody give $2 a week."* This is one of the greatest mistakes we make when talking to our students. Communicate that all of them could give $2 a week, but for many of them that would be an insult to even suggest because they spend more per week on soda pop than that.

  The other reason I don't like underchallenging is that it simply doesn't work. We waste our time and energy on something that will never happen. There will never be a time when every one of your students gives exactly $2 a week. I simply say, "Everyone needs to give something." Some of them give $1, $5, $50, or $100 a week.
- *Missions trips are not substitutes for missions giving.* A missions trip should increase your giving to missions. All young people need to go on a missions trip, and they need to raise their money on their own, just like a missionary does. This in no way should be a cop-out as to why one is not giving directly to missions.

Step 4: One Big Fundraiser

Don't waste your time doing a bunch of fundraisers that don't raise big bucks. Find one you can develop over the years that will be effective for your situation. I would rather work my tail off for one fundraiser that raises $5,000 than do five fundraisers that raise $1,000 each.

The key to success is helping people see that missions is not a fundraiser, but a face. People give to people. When we decided to give Costa Rica missionary Stan Morlin an STL van, that is when our people caught the vision. It made STL a reality. Stan Morlin responded by sending a video and saying, "Thank You!"

I suggest having one, no more than two, fundraisers a year for missions. My two big fundraisers every year were STL Sunday and the 100-hole Golf Marathon. Find out what works best with your church, because it is usually difficult to raise money for missions from the community.

Here are some fundraiser ideas:

- *STL Sunday*: one of the greatest fundraisers we did. More details in step 5.
- *100-Hole Golf Marathon*: The Northwest District sponsors this event every year. Our senior pastor golfs 100 holes in one day. I simply provide a sponsor sheet in the bulletin and make a big deal about it a couple of weeks beforehand.
- *High Gear*: This event, also sponsored by the Northwest District Youth Department, is where students and leaders raise money for a four-day bike trip.
- *Other ideas*: auctions, espresso carts, fireworks, etc. The key for you is to find one and make it big.

Step 5: STL Sunday

STL must be seen as part of the overall church missions strategy, not just a youth program. And your senior pastor must see it as a way to building missions giving in the church. I also believe it is not realistic to expect any church to live and breathe only STL. My pastor gave me two Sundays a year, and if I didn't hit a home run during these times, STL would not happen.

STL Sunday can be done any time of the year. The national date for STL Sunday is the third Sunday in October. Here are some ideas for developing your own STL Sunday:

- *Provide a quality event during a Sunday evening service.* The people in our church loved our dessert theater. We provided an illustrated message and complimentary dessert.

- *Visit adult Sunday school classes that day.* Communicate to each class the vision behind STL. Let them know about the service that evening, and give them a personal invitation.
- *Determine more than one way to raise funds that evening.* Be creative. We had five different ways that people could give to STL at the dessert theater.
- *Take an offering at the end of the message.* I preached the message and asked my senior pastor to take the offering. Our last offering was $3,500.
- *Provide a thirty-day goal card.* People were encouraged to make a goal they would fulfill in the next thirty days.
- *Do a silent auction in the back.* Before and after the event, people were able to make a bid on an item located on one of the back tables.
- *Buy a Meal.* Perhaps one of the most popular items was "Buy a Meal." People volunteered to provide a meal at someone's house one time during the year. Some payed $10 a meal, and enjoyed the fellowship with other Christians.
- *Pastors' Meal.* This was the same concept as "Buy a Meal," except the people would pay $50 for a meal with pastors. Thirty people signed up to come to my home, which raised $1,500 for STL.

The key to a successful STL Sunday is to be creative. Hit a home run on that day.

Step 6: Church Donation

STL must be more than a youth thing. The task of providing vehicles for our missionaries is bigger than students alone can accomplish. If your churches make even a small donation each year, it makes a big difference.

Step 7: Big-Day Offerings

Take special/big-day offerings. I want to encourage you to have the majority of your Sunday and midweek offerings earmarked for STL. However, set aside at least one or two days a year when you will take the biggest offering ever taken in your youth ministry.

Our junior-high Sunday school class spent one month building up to the biggest offering ever taken in their class on a Sunday morning. They worked all month collecting change and making commitments, and then they believed God. In one offering, they collected over $1,000 toward STL. Plan strategically to take big offerings throughout the year.

Step 8: Other Ideas

Here are a few more ways a church can generate STL money:

- *Add a small fee to an event.* I have talked to many youth pastors and leaders who have done this successfully. It is an easy way to generate STL funds.
- *Tithe to missions on every fundraiser.* I believe God would bless any youth ministry that puts this into effect.
- *United Way.* United Way is set up to accept any and all donations made to STL. Encourage your people who give to United Way to earmark their funds for STL.
- *Fine-time fine.* We all struggle with students not getting to the bus on time. When my wife took the youth choir on tour, every minute the students were late it was "fine time" for STL. They had to pay ten cents for every minute they were late.
- *Collect change at restaurants when you stop to eat.* Have one of your leaders go around and ask the students to give their change to STL.
- *Build missions giving over the years.* Begin with your youth right now. If I had read some of these insights earlier in my ministry, I would have grown our giving much sooner.

- *Every year, set a goal and make sure it is realistic yet challenging to the students.* It takes time to develop an STL church. In 1989, we started with giving only $2,000; by 1996, we gave over $37,000. It took a few years, but it was worth every moment.

OVERVIEW OF THE EIGHT STEPS

At this time review the eight steps we discussed. Sit down with the following chart and begin to dream a little. Ask God to open up your mind to the possibilities in your particular situation.

STL GOAL WORKSHEET

1. Youth pastor _____

2. Youth staff _____

3. Students _____

4. One fund-raiser _____

5. STL Sunday _____

6. Church donation _____

7. Big-day offerings _____

8. Other ideas _____

TOTAL _____

God has called us to make a significant difference in our world. We must think in terms of how we can impact a world with our youth ministries. We must stop and ask how we can make a difference. I am believing that in every corner of America, God will raise up youth ministries that will *win, build, and send* students to fulfill the Great Commission.

APPENDIX A

APPOINTMENT WITH GOD

A person with a disciplined devotional life can effectively answer the where, when, and how questions of his or her time with God. This sheet will help a person think through some of those questions.

DAY	TIME	PLACE
Sunday	_____	_____
Monday	_____	_____
Tuesday	_____	_____
Wednesday	_____	_____
Thursday	_____	_____
Friday	_____	_____
Saturday	_____	_____

Accountability Questions

1. Who will hold me accountable to my appointments with God?
2. What times during the week will I fast?
3. What prayer meeting will I faithfully attend every week?
4. What Bible reading plan will I personally use?

APPENDIX B

12-Minute Family Devotional Guide

1 min. *Opening prayer.*

4 min. *Read a story.* I recommend using a children's devotional book, such as *The Beginner's Devotional* by Stephen T. Barclift. The stories are great, and children love them.

2 min. *Easy questions.* Ask concrete questions to help the children think through what they just heard. The recommended devotional guide provides questions of this nature.

2 min. *Bible memorization.* Simplify a scripture down to a phrase. We enjoy using the JBQ Bible Fact-Pak for this purpose. Also, the recommended devotional guide provides scriptures to memorize.

2 min. *Prayer.* I simply have the girls and my wife lead out in a short prayer. I assign them each a specific prayer request, and I try to tie it into the story or scripture.

1 min. *Worship song.* My wife leads in one children's song we use to worship together. Don't worry about this if there is no basic music ability in your family.

Practical Helps with Family Devotions

- *Sit around the dining room table.* This helps the children to focus.
- *Decide which days you will have family devotions.* We do them on Thursday and Saturday evenings before bedtime. Don't feel pressure to do them daily.
- *We give our children nickels if they answer a question correctly or memorize a scripture.* The money is then used to buy food for hungry people in Seattle.

- *If you are a wife reading this and are frustrated with you're husband, don't put undue pressure on him.* This will only make him withdraw even more. Maybe buy him this manual and pray that this section catches his attention. Family devotions are very difficult for a man to initiate. The last thing he needs is griping from you.

APPENDIX C

BREAKTHRU YOUTH MINISTRIES
WEEKLY SCHEDULE

Sunday

9:00 A.M.   Worship service

10:30 A.M.   Junior-high Sunday school, senior-high Sunday school, Youth choir practice. Fellowship groups also meet during this time.

4:00 P.M.   Youth staff meetings (2nd and 4th Sundays), student leadership meetings (1st Sunday)

6:00 P.M.   Sunday evening church

Tuesday

7:00 P.M.   Tuesday Night Discipleship (fall and spring only)

Wednesday

3:15 P.M.   Ministers in training (MIT)

5:00 P.M.   Meal provided for everyone

5:30 P.M.   Ministry Time: phone calls, Bible quiz, worship practice, setup, drama

6:00 P.M.   Warfare prayer, Church Express, basketball and fun

6:30 P.M.   Everybody meet for prayer

6:40 P.M.   Very Important People (VIP), music and energy

7:00 P.M.   Wednesday Night Breakthru

8:30 P.M.   Altar time, hang out with and love students

Friday

6:00 P.M.   Friday Nite Hangout (2nd and 4th Fridays, fall and
              spring)
7:00 P.M.   Activities

Family Time

- Monday, Thursday, and Saturday are family nights
- Day off on Thursday

APPENDIX D

EXAMPLE OF A NEW-PERSON, MAIL-MERGE LETTER

[Month, date, year]

[First name, last name
Address
City, state, zip code]

Dear [first name]:

Thank you for your recent visit to Breakthru Youth Ministries. Our desire is to build your life. We believe in you! We want to provide a safe, high-energy place for you to grow in your relationship with Jesus Christ, and we want to help you build personal friends with students from all over this city.

Every Wednesday we come together for relevant Bible teaching, drama, music, illustrated messages, and much more! There is free pizza and soda pop for first-time guests, so invite all your friends. Free transportation is also available for those who need a ride.

[First name], we want to do everything possible to serve you. Please do not hesitate to ask questions, get involved, and make some new friends.

We believe in *you*,

Pastor Troy and Jana Jones
Youth Ministries

APPENDIX E

CAMPUS MINISTRY RESOURCES LIST

Youth Pastors Web Site

www.nwdyouth.com
"A Web site designed to provide resources and materials for youth pastors and leaders."

See You at the Pole

Promotional material
(817) 447-7526

Youth Alive

Product information
(800) 641-4319

First Priority

(615) 221-4963
Frankline, Tennessee

APPENDIX F

6:30 P.M.   Available to hang out with students
6:55 P.M.   Collect accountability sheets
7:00 P.M.   Discuss accountability sheets
7:10 P.M.   Worship and prayer
7:35 P.M.   Bible application: "What are you learning in your Bible reading time? What is God teaching you in prayer? What are you learning by taking notes on messages?"
7:50 P.M.   Bible memorization
8:05 P.M.   How-to teaching
8:20 P.M.   New assignments
8:30 P.M.   Provide refreshments and hang out until students leave

HOW-TO DISCIPLESHIP LESSONS

Here are twenty-one subjects that make excellent how-to discipleship lessons. I suggest that you cover no more than seven of these in one thirteen-week phase of discipleship. Also, rotate them between the *win*, *build*, and *send* topics.

Win

- How to reach my school for Christ
- How to win a friend to Christ
- How to pray for someone at the altar
- How to reach out to a new person
- How to win my family to Christ
- How to overcome the fear of witnessing
- How to share and write my personal testimony

176

Build

- How to grow for the rest of my life
- How to pray
- How to study my Bible
- How to fast
- How to hear God speak
- How to date
- How to give

Send

- How to unwrap my spiritual gift(s)
- How to be involved in my church
- How to know if I am called into full-time ministry
- How to operate in the gifts of the Spirit
- How to personally disciple a new believer
- How to be a campus missionary
- How to get off the bench

Appendix G

Discipleship Expectations

Pray Faithfully

- Pray at least fifteen minutes every day
- Attend Wednesday warfare prayer meeting at 6:00 P.M. each week. (If your involved in ministry, show up at 6:30.)

Become a Student of the Word

- Read the Bible every day
- Memorize Scripture assignments
- Take notes while reading
- Write three entries in your journal every week

Develop a Love for God's House

- Be on time (ten minutes early)
- Sit toward the front
- Dress nicely
- Take notes (put notes in your discipleship folder)
- Be a tither, and give to missions—such as Speed-the-Light
- Invite friends

Attend Tuesday Night Discipleship

- Be on time (ten minutes early)
- We will not tolerate any unexcused absences
- Do all assignments given
- Bring Bible, pen, notebook, and weekly accountability sheet

Be Involved with Ministry/Servanthood

- Friday Nite Hangout
- Visitation
- Bible club
- Discipling others
- And other creative ideas

Deal with Areas That Could Hinder Discipleship

- Relationships with opposite sex
- Television, music, entertainment
- Parental conflicts, family ties
- Be responsible with rides
- Sin, apathy, gossip

Appendix H

Tuesday Night Discipleship Accountability Sheet

Three Phases Minimum Commitment: Due_____

Check when completed:

I read my Bible everyday
    ❑Sun. ❑Mon. ❑Tues. ❑Wed. ❑Thurs. ❑Fri. ❑Sat.

I prayed fifteen minutes a day
    ❑Sun. ❑Mon. ❑Tues. ❑Wed. ❑Thurs. ❑Fri. ❑Sat.

❑ Memorization this week

❑ I wrote in my journal three times this week

I was on time and came with a hungry heart to:

    ❑ Wednesday warfare prayer (6:30 P.M., if in ministry)
    ❑ WNB
    ❑ Sunday morning worship (9:00 A.M.)
    ❑ Sunday school and choir

❑ I took notes on all sermons this week

❑ I am faithfully tithing and giving to missions

❑ Other assignments this week

❑ I watched _____ hours of television this week

Leader comment: _____

_____

_____

_____

Appendix I

Weekend Retreat Schedule

There are many variables to consider when planning a retreat. These will just give you some ideas.

Friday

4:00 P.M.	Load up at church
4:30 P.M.	Orientation at church
4:45 P.M.	Staff meeting at church
5:00 P.M.	Leave church. Stop for dinner on the way.
7:30 P.M.	Arrive at retreat center—free time
8:00 P.M.	Warfare prayer
8:30 P.M.	Service
11:30 P.M.	Bedtime

Saturday

8:00 A.M.	Rise and shine
9:00 A.M.	Breakfast
10:00 A.M.	Worship and workshops
12:00 P.M.	Lunch
1:00 P.M.	Free time
5:00 P.M.	Dinner
6:30 P.M.	Warfare prayer
7:00 P.M.	Service
11:30 P.M.	Bedtime

Sunday

8:00 A.M.	Rise and shine
9:00 A.M.	Breakfast

9:45 A.M.	Clean and pack up
11:00 A.M.	Final service at camp
12:00 P.M.	Lunch (sack lunch or on-the-road lunch)
1:00 P.M.	Leave camp
2:00 P.M.	Some fun activity
4:30 P.M.	Dinner provided at church
5:30 P.M.	Warfare prayer at church
6:00 P.M.	Final service at church. Include testimonies and speaker

Appendix J

Planning a Retreat

One Year in Advance

- Determine the speaker
- Reserve retreat center—lodging
- Determine the date and communicate to church office

Three Months in Advance

- Bus and van request
- Advertise to students with definite due dates
- Determine theme
- Recruit help: drivers, cooks, cabin staff, etc.
- Make a budget
- Determine worship leader
- Determine activities
- Confirm speaker and retreat center

Two Weeks in Advance

- Type out schedule
- Room assignments
- Collect permission slips and money
- Call students who haven't yet responded
- Reserve any equipment you may need (trailer, etc.)
- Put together service agenda
- Confirm bus drivers

Day of Retreat

- Relax and enjoy
- Arrive early at the church
- Make sure bus drivers and key staff arrive early
- Assign a leader to sign people in and give out room assignments
- Assign a leader to load bus
- Make sure the bus is full of gasoline

Orientation at Church

- Do your orientation before you leave church
- Begin with prayer and a short time of vision for the event
- Lay out the simple rules
- Remind everyone to use the bathroom before leaving
- Introduce leadership and cabin staff
- Have senior pastor come in and pray for the students
- Keep it short—no more than fifteen minutes

Afterward

- Write thank-yous
- Pay all your bills
- Clean bus
- Return all equipment

Appendix K

Leadership Expectations

One of the most common mistakes youth pastors and leaders make is having such high expectations that good people are turned away. We need to have expectations that release people into ministry, not limit them. The following are five expectations I had for our youth staff; I made some adjustments for support workers and student leaders.

1. *Be faithful to God:* Every leader must be faithful to his/her relationship with God. You must remember you were a Christian before you became leaders. Guard your prayer times and study the Word.
2. *Be faithful to the life of the local church.* Youth ministry is one part of life in the local church. You must be faithful to church attendance and giving of tithes and missions giving.
3. *Be faithful to students.* You must spend time weekly hanging out and calling the students.
4. *Be faithful to the youth ministry.* All youth staff must attend Wednesday Night Breakthru and Friday Nite Hangout. The goal is for every leader to find at least one area and grow in it. We all receive gifts from God, so we need to use them.
5. *Be faithful to youth staff meetings.* Training times are a must. Our youth staff meetings were the second and fourth Sundays of the month at 4:00. Student leadership meetings were the first Sunday of the month at 4:00.

Appendix L

Leadership Application

Once completed, turn the application in with a Washington State Patrol form.

Name: _____

Address: _____

City: _____ Zip Code: _____

Home Phone: (_____) _____

Date of salvation: _____

Church membership:
    ❏ Yes ❏ No

Date of water baptism _____

Special abilities/skills you have: _____
_____
_____

Which are you applying for?
    ❏ Youth staff ❏ Student leadership ❏ Adult worker

Please check yes or no. Explain on back if necessary.
1. Do you fully subscribe to the statements of faith of the Assemblies of God?
    ❏ Yes ❏ No

2. Are you presently having a consistent devotional life?
    ❏ Yes ❏ No

3. Can you work under authority, as long as it doesn't violate your Christian conscience?
    ❏ Yes ❏ No

4. Do you use tobacco, drink alcoholic beverages, or use any form of illegal drugs?
   ❑ Yes ❑ No

5. Have you ever had a problem with child abuse, either physical or sexual?
   ❑ Yes ❑ No

6. Have you ever been convicted of a criminal offense (excluding minor traffic violations)?
   ❑ Yes ❑ No

To order additional copies of

From
Survival
To
Significance

send $11.99 plus $3.95 shipping and handling to

Books, Etc.
PO Box 1406
Mukilteo, WA 98275

or have your credit card ready and call

(800) 917-BOOK

Troy Jones

Northwest District of the Assemblies of God
Phone: (425) 423-0222
email: nwdyd@ix.netcom.com
Web site: nwdyouth.com